W9-DDH-552

Television's Child

Television's Child

by Norman S. Morris

LITTLE, BROWN AND COMPANY • BOSTON • TORONTO

LIBRARY OF CONGRESS CATALOG CARD NO. 73-154952
FIRST EDITION
T08/71

Published simultaneously in Canada
by Little, Brown & Company (Canada) Limited
PRINTED IN THE UNITED STATES OF AMERICA

To the memory of my dad

Contents

Author's Note

The complications and ramifications of television for children were examined over a period of six brief months. I hope no grandchildren ever ask me to recall for them the great winter of 1970, because I must admit that, with the writing project and accompanying full-time job at CBS News, I never even observed the winter. While the focus was on children's television, the rest of the world whirled by like so many horses on a merry-go-round. Throughout this period, our friends were patient and helpful; I am grateful to them for their perseverance.

I would like to express special appreciation to Dr. Paul Syracuse and his wife, Marion, for their time, devotion and duty beyond the call; Dr. Irving Markowitz for his invaluable aid and innovative ideas; Dr. John Spillane for his psychological consultations; Dr. Jack Schwartz and his wife, Lillian, who pushed me over the roughest terrain with professional opinion and encouragement; Dr. Theodore D'Alessio, superintendent of the West Orange schools, for coming to our rescue when other educators sidestepped us; Elizabeth Wilton, director of elementary education for the West Orange schools, for her magnificent assistance in our trials with parental questionnaires; all of the parents who had the interest and courtesy to reply to those questionnaires; Paul

Taff, who provided us with clear insights into public television; Chris Dann of the A. C. Nielsen Company, who defogged the rating game for us; Bob Hatch of the Children's Television Workshop, who kept us apprised of upcoming changes; Evelyn Sarson and Lillian Ambrosino of ACT for their help in polling parents in Boston and keeping up my spirits at difficult moments; and all those who gave of their time and allowed us to interview them.

I owe also a special note of thanks to our many friends who contributed ideas and direction to our project. In particular, to Eleanor Cohen for her initial reading and criticism; Dr. Gilbert Leight for his assistance in preparing interview questionnaires and his expertise in wrestling with the fine points of English usage and grammar; Carol Beitler for helping to proof the final manuscript; Jack Gould for his guidance along the way; and the Mavins at CBS, Ed Joyce, Gerry Solomon, Rob Sunde, Jim Houtrides and Lee Otis, for making room in the work schedule to permit this book to be written.

Above all, I am most grateful to my loving wife, Sandy, who trod the whole distance by my side; our sons, Kenneth and Gregory, who are now free to take shortcuts through the den on their way elsewhere; and to my mother, who helped direct traffic around the den. Without them, I might still be at the typewriter.

Preface

In the early 1940's, an occasional television antenna sprouted from the rooftop of an affluent home. Now, three decades later, it would be easier to count the homes in America where there is not at least one TV set; multiple-set families are not uncommon. Even in homes where buying the kids a pair of shoes presents a major financial hurdle you can bet you will find one or more TV sets, and a good many of those are expensive color receivers. The last bastions of resistance crumbled before the onslaught of television when the intellectual holdouts conceded that, just as in the case of the Asian flu, no really effective inoculation against the mass medium could be found. While children are not the largest consumers of television, television is one of the largest consumers of children's time. The medium has come to rival candy and ice cream in popularity, and many parents openly encourage this popularity for its obvious benefits to themselves. When the kids get underfoot, what better and cheaper baby-sitting service than the TV set? What more convenient, inexpensive source of constant entertainment!

With so massive an infusion of information, heroes, villains, fads, fashions, stereotypes and sales promotions, it is surprising that people have not been sufficiently disturbed to find out for sure just what impact television is having on our children today. Most of what we know has been based on hearsay, and opinion on the subject is as conflicting as the testimony on "the pill."

There have been a few exceptions. In 1958, under the sponsorship of the British Nuffield Foundation, three noted psychologists (Hilde T. Himmelweit, A. N. Oppenheim and Pamela Vince) carried out a four-year study on the problem and reported in a book called *Television and the Child* (see bibliography). But the study is now almost twenty years old and many of its findings are no longer valid. Its results more nearly reflect the British culture than our own and since the investigation took place before commercial TV came to Britain the impact of British and American television is all the more difficult to compare. In this country, the Stanford sociologists, Wilbur Schramm, Jack Lyle and Edwin Parker, launched their own three-year impact study, *Television in the Lives of Our Children.* But results completed in 1961 can hardly be considered current today.

The television medium is having its own crisis. It is coming of age at an unfortunate time — at a time when we have more social unrest and turmoil than we have had in over a hundred years. And so we are resorting to one of our favorite devices, trying to look for external causes for our problems instead of looking inwardly. The television set becomes a splendid scapegoat for all our troubles. In fact, it is probably convenient *not* to have scientific answers about the medium's impact. That way we can stop asking ourselves those embarrassing questions: Am I a good parent? Am I doing the right things for my child? It is certainly easier to point to the TV set and say, "Ah, there is the villain! There lies the cause of violence in the streets."

Television, like radio before it (and like the movies before radio), is thought by many to be the major source of our troubles. When it first came along there was talk of all the permanent harm it would do to vision; that has not come to pass. We heard that television would raise havoc with school grades; that has not happened. We still hear some talk about the passivity of the medium and what it is doing to this generation. Yet has there been a more active generation in our history?

So it is not surprising that when the tides of emotion run high in this country (as they do with the subject of violence) the United States Congress will turn to examine the part television is playing in our national life. To date, three major hearings have taken place on Capitol Hill since 1951 and a fourth is underway. In the case of the three completed hearings, the conclusions were conflicting and incomplete. In each instance, there was a call for research, though no research was forthcoming. In each hearing the same experts were asked to trek back over testimony which remained inconclusive and conflicting. Meanwhile, crime in the U.S. has continued its sharp climb; violence has become with some a national pastime, and with the rest of us a national hang-up. The likelihood is that fingers will continue to point to television as a major suspect in causing the rising crime curve. The National Broadcasting Company, with good intent and partly, no doubt, in self-defense, has set about examining the possible relationship between television violence and children's behavior. That study will take five years to complete.

Violence is only one wave of the enormous spectrum of

television's impact on the child. We are concerned with other important questions as well. What is TV's effect on a child's values? How much does television actually contribute, if at all, to children's knowledge. Is the medium curtailing reading among children? To find the answers we undertook our own investigation and tried a fresh approach. Instead of relying on experts who testified before Congressional committees and who are quoted over and over again in the literature we expanded our inquiry to include new blood. Our experts included reputable clinical, not experimental, psychiatrists and psychologists. We spoke with educators in nursery and elementary schools in both the public and private sectors as well as with university educators. We interviewed network executives, television producers, TV performers and advertisers. And finally we talked to parents themselves to discover what problems they were having with television and just what questions they wanted answered.

We have attempted to pull all these points of view together in this work. In gathering all the scattered pieces of this complex puzzle, we have tried to be fair and to present a balanced picture of a most complex subject. To come to each issue with an open mind has proved to be a most difficult task. In a number of instances we have changed position from where we stood at the outset.

Another task we have set out for ourselves is to provide reasonable, flexible guidelines for parents who are confused by TV problems or are having difficulties mediating between their children and the television set. The children we have in mind are those up to the age of ten: beyond ten we are confronted with the added complexity of approaching adolescence.

We are not here to plead the case for television; neither are we attempting to structure a polemic against the medium. We happen to work for CBS News — a fact that may lead some to argue we are subject to media bias. We disclaim any such charge, recognizing that our job is to carry out the journalistic assignment of examining the state of affairs surrounding children's television and to report precisely what we find. Throughout this work the attempt is to be fair, to illuminate what is good, and to show where improvement or reform is needed. Our concern is television's impact on children: that our two young children and children in general be well served.

April 1970

Television's Child

1 HOW TELEVISION HAS RESHAPED THE CHILD'S WORLD

Some two hundred twenty-two thousand miles from earth a white glove removes a lens cap and points a television camera at a lunar crater. And in some rat-infested tenement dwelling in Harlem where the windows are all boarded up sit a group of small children, hypnotized by the image of the crater on the screen. There before them is their very own special window on the world. We call it television.

Without a doubt, television is the most powerful communications force ever created by man. Whether that force is positive, negative, or neutral *depends on what you do with it.* Television has the capacity to serve us or harm us. Whether we make the effort to harness its positive influence on our children is strictly up to us.

Television has become the major news carrier and a prime source of entertainment, superimposed on, yet intertwined with, the American culture. For grown-ups it still has a magic quality about it. We sit in our favorite living room chairs and are amazed to this day that we can observe what a lunar astronaut is doing thousands of miles away, that we can follow Joe Namath to the goal line or attend an opera in some distant city. But today's children are born into this television world and accept what it has to offer without question. It is just there — like the kitchen table or the front door — a fact of life. Children have to be taught to discriminate, to evaluate, to accept or reject television's varied input.

What Parents Believe About Children's Television

At the outset of our investigation of children's television, we wanted to know precisely what concerned the parents about this area of TV and what preconceptions they held about the impact of the medium on their youngsters. Later on we used their reactions as focal points for our discussions with our child development authorities in order to come up with appropriate answers to their questions.

We had hoped to get regional samplings to see whether there were significant differences of parental concern in different parts of the country. Unfortunately, we were unable to obtain those larger geographical samplings. Much of the difficulty arose because we found it nearly impossible to enlist the aid of educators around the nation. Many of them, in fact, failed to continue further correspondence upon learning that this was to be a private study, not supported by research grants-in-aid.

In our own area of New Jersey, parental cooperation was minimal except within the West Orange area. For months we had difficulty interviewing parents because we could not obtain the cooperation of local school boards or PTA groups. The educators, putting on their best parochial attitudes, could not see the merit of this undertaking. But educators often experience myopic vision and are unable to perceive how studies beyond the schoolyard can possibly benefit their children. Their primary concerns appear to center on such vital things as painting the school fence and making sure the broken glass on the gymnasium door is replaced. The PTAs are rarely anxious to assist in activities that may benefit their children if they have to rearrange the schedules of meetings prepared as long as thirteen months in advance. PTA leaders could not arrange for us to meet with parents, they said, because of the more urgent priorities of handling bake sales and swap shops. The same PTA officials insisted that "parents were unwilling to give up bowling nights to talk about the effects of TV on their kids." We were extremely fortunate to meet the progressive educator Dr. Theodore D'Alessio, the superintendent of the West Orange school system. He and his staff immediately saw the necessity of examining the medium and opened the school system for the preparation of this report.

Five elementary schools in West Orange totaling about two thousand students, were polled. Questionnaires were distributed to classes in kindergarten through fourth grade. Parents were also encouraged to reply in detail about their preschoolers' specific viewing habits. The director of elementary education endeavored to select schools providing a representative sampling of the West Orange community among differing economic and educational backgrounds.

Questionnaires were distributed to parents in the Boston area by members of Action for Children's Television.

In the West Orange group, more than half of the questionnaires were not returned. The Boston sampling returned amounted to approximately one-third of the distributed questionnaires.

In the survey parents were queried about their children's

reactions to television. They were asked to give impressions about such things as what seemed to frighten their children, whether youngsters appeared to have any reaction to the assassinations of the Kennedy brothers and Dr. Martin Luther King, and what shows seemed to appeal to the children. The interviews also probed the use families were or were not making of television. Were parents, for instance, attempting to provide proper supervision of the programs or using the set purely as an inexpensive baby-sitter. The survey also attempted to discover whether television presented conflicts over homework, meals or bedtime routines. And finally the interviews tried to find out what kinds of programs they would like television to provide for young people.

Measuring Television's Impact

In trying to understand TV's impact on children one thing cannot be overstressed. Television is a tremendous force, but it is only one influence in a child's life. We tend often to brush aside the effect of peer pressures, social relationships, and individual needs. Yet the older a child gets the less television influences him, and the more these other factors in life take over. On the other hand, the young child is an animated, talking sponge. Whatever he sees or hears he soaks up indiscriminately. Children have the ability to absorb information long before they are able to talk, a fact parents often overlook. They will place an infant in front of a television screen to amuse him and provide themselves with some free time, but they do not stop to *wonder about* the TV impressions that may be swallowed whole. One of the distinguishing characteristics of television is its all-commanding presence. It demands attention from both eyes and ears, and it focuses attention on movement within a small area. The screen may be beside the dining room table, in the living room, or wherever considered most convenient, but all of the conditions for attention and absorption are built right into the set. Some things are discarded, some things are retained, and the final product is what we call television's influence or impact on the child.

The primary obstacle in measuring impact is the almost impossible job of isolating the television experience from all the other factors that impinge on the child's life. The same television experience will affect two people differently, and this fact alone helps to explain the great difficulty in studying impact. You simply cannot reproduce in a laboratory experiment the conditions of real-life situations; this is one of the major problems of research psychology. The evidence studied by various Congressional blue ribbon committees on violence has been based on such tenuous experiments and is certainly open to question. Indeed, we have reason to believe that the originators of some of those oft-quoted experiments are fully aware that they have sold this bill of goods in exchange for various scientific grants-in-aid. That is why this investigation will go beyond the walls of the research laboratory, and that is why our evidence comes not from academicians but from clinicians who see children in action every day.

Television and the Nuclear Family

One of the cultural phenomena of this atomic age has been the development of the nuclear family — typically the father-mother family with two children isolated in a city apartment or out in the suburbs. As psychiatrist Irving Markowitz, medical director of the Family Service and Child Guidance Clinic in East Orange, New Jersey, has pointed out, in the nuclear family you derive your pleasures from within a tight family structure, and the nuclear family openly encourages more use of the TV set. Mobility in our transient society has scattered the extended family (parents and children together with aunts, uncles, and grandparents) and stretched, then broken it into small nuclear family units. When extended families were more likely to live together, the kids did not have to look to their parents for all of their entertainment. There were the uncles and grandparents nearby who helped to divert and amuse them. A child's entertainment was more diffused. Today's parents, who are called upon to do the lion's share of the entertaining, abdicate to the television set. The suburban nuclear family has the additional problem of transportation. Driving to the movies or driving the kids over to see their friends becomes a drag, and the simple solution is to drop the children in front of the television set for wall-to-wall entertainment. Some parents acquire feelings of guilt. What we have, then, is a good deal of talk about the harm all that television viewing is doing to the kids, with the people who make it all possible doing most of the talking.

What About the Competition?

In the old days (before television), the kids' domain was outdoors — summer or winter. Occasionally they had to be pried out, but once they were there it was tough getting them to come in. You would yell, "Supper's ready!" and wind up organizing a search party that headed for the playground or alongside the creek. Children loved to take long walks with their friends, build orange-crate scooters, dip their hands into a bowl of papier-mâché. All this has changed. There is that electronic box forever calling to them to come inside, and the job of marching the kids outside again takes renewed effort. From the child's standpoint it is easier to plop down on the floor and be entertained, and it is easier for the parent to allow this to happen than it is to keep thinking up constructive things for them to do. In this never-ending tug-of-war other activities are curtailed in favor of TV viewing.

Television has changed play patterns, and they in turn have altered relationships between friends. In the past, you would wait for a small neighbor to drop by on rainy days, and the two of you would launch some project. Now television has become a kind of playmate substitute, and kids are apt to content themselves with watching the tube rather than wandering out in the rain in search of companionship. Television has diluted relationships to such an extent that very young people seem less dependent on each other for friendship.

The TV set has also diluted the relationship between the child and his parents. In one sense, it provides us with an "out" when we are beat. When we have had a rough day at the office or when everything has gone wrong in the house and there are the kids buzzing in our ears at the culmination of it all, we can simply turn to them and say, "Why don't you go find something to watch!" But in another, very real sense we can also view the TV set as a competitor for our attention. At times we can feel strong resentment of television. Before the days of television, a child would come to his parents and say, "What can I do?" and usually they would find him something to do. These days, if we are in the midst of something and our kids chime in with a request that we find busy work for them, more often than not they are directed to the television set. We may go to them later and suggest they join us and go for a ride. And we are annoyed to hear our six-year-old tell us he would really prefer watching Misterogers. Is it because we love our children any less than our parents loved us? Is it because our children love us any less than we did our parents? No, but it is true that parent-child relationships are becoming more diffused and television is assisting in the process.

Instant History

When we old-timers (those of us past thirty) went to school, most of what we learned about history still came from books and magazines. But there is a new kind of history. Today, and every day, children are being exposed to electronic history, are watching it take form and dimension on the television screen. It is a process that simultaneously molds the thinking of young viewers and transforms them into the more sophisticated generation they are.

Crooked politics, dirty air, and street muggings are nothing new. But they were not always discovered right away. And they certainly were not issues for kids. Not so long ago about the only thing a kid knew about a newspaper was that he was told to bring it off the front porch. He might make off with the comic page. But now that instant history is with us older children find out about these things at once. It makes them uptight about the quality of American life and American institutions. It is reasonable to assume that this instant history learning is having some effect on younger brothers and sisters. It is a situation that makes parents uptight, too, because there is often the underlying feeling that children should be protected from life.

3R + TV = Think² or What TV Is Doing to Education

The overwhelming majority of mothers and fathers are convinced that television is changing the quality of their children's education. There is a very positive feeling that preschoolers are entering the school systems at much more advanced levels than young children ever did before the advent of TV. Some educators are already predicting that this onrush of knowledge advanced by such programs as *Sesame Street* could force school systems to upgrade the curricula for the early grades.

Throughout the country *Sesame Street* has been warmly applauded in middle-class homes. Its sophisticated blend of basic learning skills with good-natured wit and skillful artwork makes it appealing not only to preschoolers but to schoolchildren and parents as well. The producers of the program, the Children's Television Workshop, are working hard to close the gap between the preschool experience of middle-class children and that of those in the ghetto. On the presumption that disadvantaged preschoolers do not have much exposure to educational TV, the Children's Workshop has sought ways to publicize *Sesame Street* and plug the program into day-care centers and Head Start projects. To accompish this, the workshop resorted to stuffing promotional leaflets into shopping bags, phone bills, and welfare check envelopes. Posters advertising *Sesame Street* were put up in neighborhood barbershops and churches. From all indications, the slow process of publicizing the program in the "disadvantaged" neighborhoods began to pay dividends in audience build-up in the inner city.

In West Orange, teachers we have interviewed believe television is compelling them to alter their classroom methods. Some traditional educators persist in saying television cannot offer a child new knowledge. Their viewpoint is that the ephemeral nature of the medium prevents it from dispersing any significant information in depth.

From Boxtops to Barbies

In the Crackerjack and Jack Armstrong generations, one of life's great temptations was to empty the contents from the box of breakfast cereal before anybody had a chance to consume the food. The point was to find a tiny trinket or perhaps a whistle hidden in the box. But more often than not we were after the boxtop so we could send away for a decoder ring or a Dick Tracy badge. Our idea of prizes was certainly not very grandiose.

Soaps were familiar to us; so were toothpastes. These, however, were sold to our parents, never directly to us as children. And soaps and toothpastes just about comprised our total knowledge of consumer products. What a contrast to today's product-conscious children! Merchandise of every conceivable description cascades into the living room. Racing cars (one model number after another), dolls that talk, walk, skate and grow teeth (many costing up to $25), and an assortment of toys, toothpastes, cereals and candy are sold incessantly. Children are learning to read from television, and the first words they recognize are often product names.

"Jell-O!" a four-year-old cries out in the supermarket, to the astonishment of his mother. But what is all of this doing to children's values?

So Near Yet So Far

The great promise of television was that it would draw people together, that it would connect remote regions of the world. In one way, this has happened. We can see an event on the evening news that occurred in Paris, London, or Saigon on the very day it happened, and we may tell ourselves that television allows us to become more involved in what is taking place elsewhere. This is Marshall McLuhan's view. However, "Marshall McLuhan," says psychiatrist Irving Markowitz, "holds a very optimistic notion, but one I think is optimistic to the extreme. McLuhan is convinced that we'll really smell the other guy's problems over the TV set, that electronic contact will decrease remoteness. Unfortunately, it does not work that way; the remoteness is even greater. In other words, we now have a way of perusing what's going on without having to get our feet in the mud."

Parents very often have ambivalent feelings about television and may experience a gnawing uncertainty about what TV is doing to children. As with so many other fears some of this is simply fear of the unknown. We were not raised on television, so we do not know how to deal with it.

But parents should not automatically assume that the influence of television on their children is comparable to the impact of radio in their childhood. The TV impact is infinitely more involved in a much more complicated world.

2 THE CREDIBILITY QUESTION: DO CHILDREN BELIEVE TV MIRRORS LIFE?

Mark Twain once wrote, "A baby is an inestimable blessing and a bother." Probably that is the way most parents feel and have always felt. After all, kids take up a lot of time and as soon as they are fairly ambulatory and reasonably vocal we say to them, "How's about shoving off and finding something to do — preferably outside?" Within this context the TV set when it came along presented quite a boon. If the child could not think of any place to go or began that all-too-familiar game called "insees and outsees" we would say, "Oh, go watch TV." Many parents just disregard step one and send the kid straight to the television set, there to be amused and out of their hair. The images that flow across the screen are sometimes familiar to the parent, but just how children perceive what they are watching is not generally understood or given much thought. Many grown-ups assume, and assume incorrectly, that kids see the same way they do.

Television programmers, strangely enough, generally have no greater understanding about how children perceive than the rest of us. Yet they would have us convinced that they do, and there they sit devising new programs for kids. One case in point comes to mind. A network executive kept arguing with us that children are acutely perceptive. "You can't fool me for one minute," he told us. "Kids are undersold all the time. They can tell what's real and what's not real anytime." And an advertising executive in charge of one of the largest toy accounts remarked, "Kids are foolproof. You can snow adults, but even the littlest children can tell fantasy from reality." Well, it can all sound terribly convincing when you are sitting there in some executive suite. The voices all sound so authoritative, and it is only when you leave that it begins to dawn on you that you have just witnessed some fancy executive footwork and that a lot of your questions really have not been answered at all.

What the programmer and advertiser have done is to lump age groups together. They talk about "children," but what children? You cannot reasonably equate the perception of a two-year-old with that of a ten-year-old then quickly add that little kids are just a little less knowledgeable than older ones. It is a delusion for people to reason that all children can separate the real from the unreal strictly on the basis of the way young people happen to feel and think. It is a good deal more complex than that. When the question was put to our battery of psychiatrists and psychologists, it became apparent immediately that we had opened a can of worms.

Fantasy and Reality

Fantasy, as psychiatrist Paul Syracuse explains, begins very early in life. Dr. Syracuse, who sees a lot of children in his practice in the Greater New York area, says in some cases kids begin fantasizing even before they can talk. In fact, it is often hard to get kids' attention just because they are fantasizing so much and so rapidly. "Charlie," we may call, but

Charlie does not come. We may think that he is deliberately disobeying us or that he has a hearing problem. But probably he is so busy fantasizing he is literally in some other world. Is this bad? Something for us to grow concerned about? Not at all. Fantasizing is quite useful. It enables Charlie and at times all the rest of us to discharge or accomplish through imagination what we are unable to do in reality. "Wouldn't it be nice," we can tell ourselves when the boss is hitting us over the head, "if we could just fly away?" It is a fantasy that enables us as adults very often to cope with some unpleasant situations.

Fantasy begins when we are infants. Child psychiatrist Irving Markowitz says a child below the age of three views life in isolated sequences. When he looks at a television set, according to Dr. Markowitz, the child does not see a flow of events. His television perception is one of disjointed, isolated sequences and so is his reality. When for example, the child walks down the street and sees two people holding hands, he may focus on that. In the sense of observing objects in sequences, there is no credibility gap between the child's sense of reality and what he views on the screen. "You can't talk about a perceptual defect in this young child," Dr. Markowitz adds, "and say it interferes with his fantasy formation. It comes down to this: his way of perceiving reality or fantasy is simply peculiar to that age." A child's fantasy is not a distortion of his perception. With respect to television viewing, he has a fantasy when what he sees on the screen is not something he can identify with in his own personal life. That is the fantasy of a very young child.

Between the ages of three and four children weld those isolated sequences together and are able to follow a story line. You can see a forecast of this when the child asks repeatedly, "What's happening?" Finally, he may come and tell us about the story. But the fact that the child can follow a simple story line raises a question as to whether he is, at the same time, able to tell whether what he sees is reality or fantasy.

To understand this, look at the television set. It has a knob which you can turn on or off. The child of three or four knows the knob is real. But he wonders where the picture goes when the set is turned off. His conclusion probably is that it goes to the back of the set. "In a sense," says Dr. Markowitz, "to the child the story is still going on." That makes it difficult for him to differentiate between reality and fantasy. The knob is real but the feeling that the story goes on is confusing and fuzzes the situation. Misterogers (*Misterogers' Neighborhood*) tells the story of a child of nearly four who met him in the lobby of a New York hotel and inquired, "How did you get out of the set, Misterogers?" Fred Rogers patiently explained that television was only a kind of picture that moved. The little boy nodded his head as though he comprehended perfectly, then asked, "But Misterogers, how are you going to get back into the television set?"

So the three- or four-year-old child is experiencing some difficulty telling what is real and what is not. In some mystical way he feels the story within the TV tube is continuing. The form of a television program, though, can sometimes help. For example a child can look at a cartoon and know that it is not real. Even the youngest children have had some experience drawing or using crayons, and when they view a cartoon on television they see it as a drawing that moves. When a child sees a picture of Snow White in a book, that for him is a kind of cartoon drawing. The television version of Snow White is also a cartoon drawing, the difference being that it projects action. The child can look around at his mother and say to himself, "She is real, and this thing on the TV set — this cartoon — is not like my mother; therefore, it's not real." But does the child think that this moving cartoon drawing continues when he turns the real knob off, much the way he may believe other TV stories go on in the back of the tube? "No," answers Dr. Markowitz. "In this case, the three- or four-year-old believes the cartoon drawings go back into the bottle of ink. After all, that's where they came from in the first place." The child will not confuse cartoons with reality because they are so contrary to his everyday experience.

Boston psychiatrist John B. Spillane believes the western is another dramatic form that helps children of this age draw distinctions between fantasy and reality. Kids observe the broad, stylized kind of acting in the melodramas and realize that it is not true to life. Even before young children can talk, they are adept at picking up facial cues from grown-ups around them in order to judge reactions. In westerns realistic cues on the faces of the actors for the most part are missing. Furthermore, westerns take place in geographical settings that are completely foreign to the child in his present environment and this, too, in Dr. Spillane's opinion, helps the child to recognize the western as fantasy. Merely living with the TV set in the house helps the child develop distinctions between fantasy and reality. He comes to understand that the on-and-off switch provides him with some control over the picture on the tube. And this control factor gradually weans the child away from his acceptance of the television picture as reality.

For children somewhere between five and seven years of age, the question of whether any specific program on television is real or not becomes much more clearly defined, as the following illustration will show:

Jack and Richard, two six-year-olds, were playing down in the basement of Jack's house one afternoon when, apparently apropos of nothing in particular, Jack ran upstairs.

"Mom, how does Pixanne fly?"

(Pixanne is a television counterpart of Peter Pan and until recently she lived in a magic forest syndicated in a number of cities by Metromedia.)

The little boy's mother noted the urgency in the tone of his question. "You know how she flies, Jack," she replied. "Why are you asking?"

"Well, I just wanted you to tell me."

His mother thought for a minute, then said, "If you really want to know — she flies by wire."

"But she said she flies by fairy dust," came the distressed voice.

By this time Jack's companion, Richard, had joined them and decided to put his two cents in. "Oh, there's no such thing as fairy dust. She uses a wire."

"She does not!" Jack shot back in anger.

"She does so. She uses a wire. There ain't no such thing as fairy dust."

Jack burst into tears. The debate went on for more than an hour. While Richard was content to accept the reality of flight by wire, Jack fought hard not to accept something he really had begun deep down to suspect.

This episode illustrates just what is happening in the lives of children who are about the age of six. They themselves are beginning to draw firm lines separating fantasy from reality. The process evolves gently at this stage of development, and there is a tendency for confusion to crop up now and again until suddenly it seems to lock into place. In Richard's case the distinction between fantasy and reality was firmly established, but Jack was still experiencing a little trouble.

Once the child has become sufficiently experienced in life and has mastered the ability to distinguish between what is real and what is not, we may say that he has begun to sprout the seedlings of mature judgment. Six-and-a-half-year-old Everett sat quietly through the CBS Children's Hour production of *Summer Is Forever* and was quite moved by the play. At the conclusion he turned to his father and remarked, "That story isn't real, Dad. But it *could* have been."

We accept things as real when we can relate them to experiences in our own lives. We can take a fantasy figure and authenticate it by linking it to something real in our own experience. Santa Claus, for example, is a fantasy figure that we authenticate by leaving presents around. What we are doing with the Santa Claus myth is blurring fantasy with real experience. Very often, in this way, adults *deliberately blur the fantasy and reality images* for a child. Sometimes we do it because we find the child's reality is too harsh. We may try to spare him by treating his fantasy as though it were reality. On television we may deliberately blur fantasy and reality by introducing warm people together with an assortment of puppets to produce a secure, pleasant environment. In teaching small children by TV the idea is to create a receptive environment for learning by transporting children from a threatening atmosphere to one that is, for the time being at least, pleasant. Attempts to do this are being made by programs like *Sesame Street* which purposely blur reality with fantasy.

Parents should be aware that blurring does occur, that usually it is part of the child's development, but that it can also occur because the television producers stimulate confusion either deliberately or unawares. The parents' job, therefore, is to be at hand whenever possible and certainly alert to help the child draw lines between fantasy and reality whenever confusion arises.

How Dead Is Dead?

Over a Bloody Mary at New York's Hotel Americana movie and television critic Judith Crist remarked to us that death portrayed on TV loses its meaning. She was saying that kids see a television character die on one program, and — lo and behold — he is miraculously reincarnated on a panel show. The kids, Mrs. Crist went on, know that TV death — with the exception of death shown on the news — is a put-on. The implication is that all the deaths on television — and we will leave the exact count of those to the antiviolence crowd — are inuring children to the concept of suffering and death. But when you talk about children and their conceptualization of death, again you can not lump together the death concept of a two-year-old with that of an older child.

In our interviews with parents many of them told us that their very young kids were terribly upset whenever they watched people dying in television plays. Barry Bricklin, a clinical psychologist in Philadelphia, explains that these are the parents who are attributing their own emotional reactions and hang-ups to their kids. "This is one of the greatest mistakes parents make," says Dr. Bricklin. "When the mother or father attributes upset to the child, what they are really telling us is that *they* were upset."

The idea of finality in death is grasped by children when they are somewhere between seven and nine. Before then, death is a reversible process. Here is how psychiatrist John Spillane describes the way young people look at it:

"I suppose the questions about death come up when the child is about three and a half or four. That's when they begin struggling with the problem of extinction. They may ask questions along this line about their pets. 'Will my cat or dog die?' and so forth. When a child of this age looks at television and sees a dead soldier, for instance, he believes that although this soldier is dead, he nevertheless returns."

This helps to explain why cartoon violence really does not upset the child. The rabbit falls off the cliff, hits bottom and — in keeping with the child's reversible death concept — is restored. No damage has been done to the child's psyche because that is the way he sees death.

As the child grows older, he gets somewhat acquainted with death's finality even in his own backyard. He may step on an ant or caterpillar and find that it no longer moves. It is *dead,* and he begins to plant this idea somewhere in his subconscious. Of course, a death close to the child (in his family, for instance) may hasten the process. But even if this does not take place, the concept settles in between the ages of seven and nine. An older child has no problem accepting cartoon deaths because by the time he has dismissed the reversible idea of death he has become used to the convention of the film cartoon.

Many of us have had a small child point a toy gun in our direction and say, "Bang! You're dead!" At such times we may say to ourselves, this kid's parents had better teach him a thing or two, because when he grows up he'll be pointing a real gun at somebody. Is he an exception to the rule? Does he have an awareness of the finality of death? Not at all. Writing in the *New York Times Magazine* in September 1969 ("The Violent Bugs Bunny"), the chairman of the department of psychiatry at the University of Hawaii Medical School, John F. McDermott, offers the following explanation: "The angry child who says, 'I wish you were dead' really means, 'I wish you would go away because you bother me and I can't cope with you in actuality.' "

Then we come to grips with the horror of death in the older children. This is not something the child conjures up; it is a reaction parents project.

"Kids accept death," comments Dr. Markowitz. "It is only that we build up the horror. But kids don't have a posterity value in terms of their being necessary to the survival of another person. Therefore, in a sense, death isn't important to kids. When does it become important? When you have somebody else dependent on you. You have a function then, in the sense of having to keep somebody else alive. You are not allowed to die. The mortgage won't get paid. If a kid dies, the mortgage still gets paid. He knows it. So it's very practical and he doesn't have that sense of importance. The only importance he has is that he may be betraying his parents who've made such an investment in him, and he may be important to them. But the kid feels he does not have the same importance he would have as an adult, so death doesn't mean that much to kids."

When you talk about television death, that is not something that hits the child hard. The kind of death that may strike home would be the portrayal of the killing of a pet animal, because that has a good deal more meaning for young people.

So once again the problem comes right down to us. When the little kids are looking at the news and viewing the horror and tragedy of rioting and war it is not our job to put a blindfold on them. What we *should* be doing is helping them to understand the realities and values of life and helping them to grow. We do this in part by pointing out the consequences and suffering that death brings.

All for the Price of One Admission

In times like these, when people worry about such things as bombs and clean air, it is not surprising that some thought should be given to the issue of just how contaminated the television airways are with questionable values. Of course, when you are thinking in terms of a very young, impressionable audience, the question of the values transmitted takes on added proportions. Mature adults should certainly be equipped to deal with questionable values, but small children present quite another problem. Nobody can seriously doubt that commercials are crammed with all sorts of messages aside from the sales pitch, but a good deal of the time we just do not pay much attention to the extraneous value messages. Whether a given child will let them pass or absorb them depends a lot on how much or how little he gets from the adults around him. The values transmitted in commercials take on added significance because the child accepts the sales pitch as real. Unless a parent helps filter out as much of the concomitant value static as possible, the probability is quite high that the child will also accept that drivel as real, too.

These values come in three flavors: blatant, subtle and subliminal. The child is between three and a half and four when he is first able to recognize the commercial *as* a commercial, but kids remain pretty susceptible to the wild claims of Madison Avenue even up to the age of ten or more. Parental or adult supervision can offer the only effective serum against phony values.

For the introduction of undesirable values, the innocent-appearing commercial can be an insidious vehicle. Let us say you are watching a commercial and you tell the child that the product is worthless for such and such a reason. Well, you may have thought you presented a convincing argument; that ends that, and he will not pick up anything else. Your words were probably directed against the *product itself* and *not* against the shoddy techniques used to sell it. So the more treacherous values slip by and the child may conceivably absorb them.

To illustrate the point, it is, as Dr. Markowitz points out, possible to teach people to condone violence, and it can be done without showing the slightest hint of gore. One method that works beautifully is to introduce the notion of superiority. If you say that all Americans have a right, by any means, such as by Americanism, to accomplish some particular objective, you are providing automatic condonation of force to instill it. What you say is that your motives are so good that any damn fool should accept them. Now of course this is a very subtle way of teaching that "might makes right," but it is also very effective. It is much more encouraging of violence, in fact, than displaying a repetition of violent action itself. Interestingly enough, Dr. Irving Markowitz says that rape is also the same thing; it is a disguised example of this idea that might makes right, and it has nothing to do with sex! The rapist is the guy who says, "I am so good, so beautiful, nobody recognizes it and I am going to prove it. Whatever I do is fine because it is good and beautiful"; and he says to his victim, "If *you* do not accept it, I will overcome you."

A mother can look at the television set and be terribly concerned whether a commercial her child sees shows skirts that are too short. But what she lets slip by without question perhaps is the male chauvinism that flows from the TV tube like wine. According to Dr. Markowitz, the message that gets through so often is this: "Look, kid! It is O.K. for men to manhandle women and to fight among themselves; but as long as you are a kid, as far as these two things are concerned, that is off limits. But later . . . !" In any number of subtle ways, television teaches kids that women are to be ogled at and treated as objects, and it actually is a severely antifeminist viewpoint that comes through.

Television commercials also put a good deal of subliminal stress on pure and simple connivance to justify all sorts of cultural values that are basically corrupt. You see it in such things as the word "good," which comes to mean the right hair oil, the right deodorant, the right toothpaste. The idea is to use the right goo and you get the right guy. We are part of a great success-oriented culture. It is something to be striven for at all cost. The question Dr. Markowitz puts to us here is: "Should we allow our kids to be sold the idea that success has nothing to do with intrinsic worth or virtue, but that proper manipulation can bring about success?"

Can TV Influence a Child's Taste?

Psychiatrist Paul Syracuse remarks, "Unless the parent exercises some control over the TV set, I don't see how television *couldn't* influence a kid's taste."

A confirmation from Dr. Markowitz:

"I think one thing TV does do is give a child a real taste of affluence. There's a greater variety of things presented to him on the tube. Long ago a kid wouldn't question one family car; now he sees his family with two and sometimes more cars — lots of gadgets on them, too. Look at toys! They're much more opulent, and I think kids get the notion, 'Hey, look at those new models. Boy! *That's* around!' And you see it in their play all the time. 'Gee whiz! *He's* got that kind of football!' 'You should see *his* racing car!' 'I like the new kite the kid next door has.' Of course television can influence their taste — and it does!"

So by now it should be abundantly clear that the television medium is quite capable of transmitting values and taste along with product information and program material. Should we now wring our hands and toss the set in the rubbish? Well, we do not have to get quite so dramatic. After all, television is only *one* influence on a child's life, albeit a strong voice. But so are the voices of playmates and friends. Parents know almost instinctively that the way to counteract the harmful influences of peer pressure is to do an effective job in instilling the values they accept and believe in. Unwanted television values can be overridden in the same manner. It is a matter of gradually increasing the child's awareness of value messages that are piggybacked atop sales messages. If the parent detects unsavory messages slipping in, he should not ignore them but bring them out into the open and discuss them. That is the surest way of keeping harmful values from being swallowed whole by children.

Whether children do or do not believe that television mirrors life sounds like a deceptively simple question. We have seen that the answer depends on the age of the child we have in mind. Children around three or so take in what they view on television as part of their reality; they have no way of distinguishing yet between a real and a make-believe world.

Somewhat older children, between three and five, are now beginning to separate portions of what they see as real from what they view as unreal. They anchor their reality, defining it in terms of their own personal life experiences.

At about the time they go to school, between five and seven, they are learning to discriminate. Psychologist Barry Bricklin points out that these children know their fathers do not act like people on the *Beverly Hillbillies* and that fathers do not always act as nicely as Fred MacMurray does toward his TV kids. By this time they know these are stories. They can now accept the idea that such things as news, space shots and sports events belong to the real world, while most of the other fare lies in the realm of fiction.

For children who are six and older, who have little or no

difficulty telling what is representative of real life and what is not, commercials often present a real problem. These children readily accept the product advertised as part of the real world, but they are also susceptible to absorbing the questionable, often false values that accompany the advertised message. Indeed, many adults have degrees of this susceptibility themselves.

3 OF MICE AND MEN

Within a few short blocks of one another three tall Manhattan buildings reach heavenward like giants in silent devotion. The prayers emanating from each are for the highest rating figures possible for their respective programs. Here at the New York headquarters of ABC, CBS, and NBC, the guiding spirits behind each of the networks put in long, arduous hours to make their individual prayers come true in an atmosphere of frantic rivalry. Some of the fiercest competition these days is taking place in children's programming — especially during the Saturday morning cartoon block. And the men responsible for grabbing the largest shares of the available young TV audience often gaze down into the streets far below, brooding over the unpredictable viewing habits of the audience they often refer to as "the mice."

The Decision Makers

For more than two decades children's television has orbited on the dark side of the medium. Throughout that long period of time, bright but brief flashes of quality illuminated the children's area, yet the intrinsic significance of children's programming largely went unnoticed. Whatever sparks streaked through the darkness were the products of the abrasive, creative energies of a very few, remarkable people in television. Eventually these sporadic creative pulsars awakened the upper echelon of TV decision makers to the commercial potentials of a virtually untapped young audience. And what burst forth on the screen as a result was not a stream of truly imaginative, often costly shows for children but the profitable Saturday morning cartoon blossom. The cartoon block, as it has come to be known, arouses a sense of the hunt in many television officials who thirst for a good competitive economic battle with the opposition.

So much publicity has been given the Saturday block that the temptation among many has been to equate the entire range of children's programming with the Saturday shows. The equation is all the more unfortunate because it somehow nudges all children's shows into the economic spotlight, and the definition of a "successful show" becomes one that is bathed in dollars and ratings, not one that meets the emotional and/or intellectual needs of youngsters. That being the case, it is not too difficult to understand why those who are charged with the final decisions in the children's area are the officials with business acumen.

The assumption is that in commercial television children's programs come under the aegis of corporate businessmen. These are the officials who hold such titles as vice president of daytime programming or vice president of TV programming. Traditionally, the responsibilities of such officials have been the overseeing of afternoon and evening adult programs, and the careful placement or displacement of shows to keep network overall ratings as high as possible. Their major efforts are directed toward the rigorous job of audience building. But somehow children's programming was thrust under their wings, probably because nobody in the corporate structure could decide who else should be responsible for the young audience.

This corporate organizational move may build a broader power base for the individual vice president, but at the same time it creates problems. In the case of the official, it places an enormous burden he obviously cannot carry alone. There are not sufficient hours in a day to devote to a programming sector that is infinitely complicated. Beyond that, the programmer may or may not be interested in children aside from the economic leverage their shows may offer him. On the one hand, he may be somewhat knowledgeable about their needs; on the other, he may be abysmally ignorant. Either way, young people are being shortchanged. It is a mistake to consider the children's audience a diminutive adult audience and to lump it under daytime programming simply out of economic expediency.

There are a good many different audiences within the children's group, all with varying views, all with varying perceptions. The children's group demands its own specialist who knows kids the way a programmer knows ratings, an individual who is concerned about young children. What is needed at each network is not a titled executive who reports to a daytime programmer, not a "director" who does not have complete autonomy, but a man who stands on equal footing with the programmer. In short, what is essential is a vice president for children's programming who reports *directly to top management only,* somebody at the helm who can say with authority and backing, "I don't want to look at the rating book, I don't want to look at the cost per thousand. I have a good program here for the kids. Put it on!"

Getting There Is Half the Fun

Program executives are easily reached when a network would like to publicize one of its new shows, but when a reporter requests a general interview with the decision maker of children's television, that is quite another matter. Some attempt is made to determine whether the reporter is "sincere," which means whether he has come with hostile intent to ask embarrassing questions about the full lineup of kids' programs. Many of the people who make these interview arrangements are extremely sensitive to the intent of the proposed conversations, and some are completely unwilling to risk unfavorable publicity. The American Broadcasting Company's voice is not heard in this book because the network assiduously avoided setting up an interview appointment. Over a period of four months, frequent calls were placed to ABC's programming department, whose executives were "in meetings" or "out of town"; no calls were ever returned. One can therefore judge ABC's attitude toward its children's audience only by what appears on the screen. ABC offers something like four straight hours of cartoons on Saturday mornings, and two hours on Sundays, most of them of the poorest quality. Their one promising contribution, called *Discovery,* comes at a low viewing point on Sunday mornings. The title suggests not only the program content but also the limited chance that interested viewers can find the show in the time slot allotted. ABC, however, has not lost sight of the economic potential of the children's audience. It moved *Dark Shadows,* a bizarre soap opera featuring vampires, ghouls and monsters, from 3:30 P.M. (EST) to 4:00 P.M. to pick up the huge segment of children returning from school. One must assume ABC finds *Dark Shadows* a very entertaining family show. Game manufacturer Milton Bradley has not overlooked the appeal *Dark Shadows* has for children. The company has developed and marketed a game called Barnabas Collins, which is based on the vampire character starring in the ABC television soap opera.

Thirty-fourth Floor, Please!

They call the place Blackrock. All four sides of the huge CBS structure are faced in unrelieved black granite. It has a cold look about it, the perfect corporate edifice, the uniformity of a super highway tilted to a vertical position. The wood-paneled interiors, laminates, and diffused fluorescent lighting do nothing to add warmth to the interior. Floors are color-coded; even ashtrays match. If one inadvertently picks up the wrong color ashtray, the next morning the proper one is put back in place by unseen hands. Pictures are not hung in offices without permission from an official decorating committee. And in this setting flourish some of the most creative, nonconformist minds in the television business, a fact that is even more stark than the surroundings.

Mike Dann's desk was near a large floor-to-ceiling window. This programmer could glance to the right and see below him the distant horizon and a big chunk of New York City.

"Mr. Dann, you're in charge of television programming for CBS. But can you spell out your background in the children's area?"

"I was a child," he began, "and I have children, and I

care about them. I care about all children. I find the most rewarding experiences for children come from certain TV programming."

He talked about how his own children enjoyed and learned about politics from television. His nine-year-old, for instance, had been completely captivated by the televised political conventions.

"Children are terribly fascinated by actuality," Dann continued. "Young people have amazing interest in the immediacy of the medium — they love to see an event as it is happening."

Mike Dann impresses you as a straight shooter — very sharp. He has a youngish face with grayish-white hair, the air of a man who has been around and who knows his way.

"What would you say about the values that kids get through TV?"

"Well, I think children get true values and real values from television. Certainly more than from the comic strip."

But, as we have seen in the previous chapter, the values that stream in may not be precisely the ones you would want *your* children to pick up. Interestingly, Dann reported that as his own children were growing up he did not permit them to view programs during the week. Moreover, they were not allowed to play basketball during the week either. He said they were compelled to do something more intellectually alive.

"Aren't there times, Mr. Dann, when as a programmer you feel caught in a conflict between pressures of the budget and a desire for putting on a better show?"

"Well, it does lead to embarrassment at times. I'm not always proud of the programs I put on the air. But it isn't because I haven't tried. I think embarrassment isn't perhaps the word. It's the sense of personal failure. I feel bad when I haven't succeeded. I think I have a feeling of guilt when I have failed. I think I have never consciously tried to put on a program that I thought was wrong. And yet I have put on programs that were certainly open to question. The impact of television on children is something we're studying. We just don't know very much about it. But I would say it's certainly accurate to say that I'm not so much embarrassed, as I have a sense of failure."

(Weeks after this conversation with Mike Dann I recalled his honesty, when Judith Crist said to me, "I think Mr. Dann has been intelligent and I credit him with openness. He'll say such and such is off the record when it is, but he won't lie to you on or off the record. He has done good thinking and good planning.")

The CBS vice president spoke at some length about the harshness of the rating game. Finally, he looked at me hard and said, "You know, the theory behind ratings is really pretty simple. Commercial television essentially programs for most of the people most of the time. But what it comes down to is that *I* always try to do good things while I try to please the people."

Does Mike Dann see something of a programming void for children between six and ten?

"Well, you know, CBS has *Captain Kangaroo*. We are the only network that, on a daily basis, caters to children at all! When you are talking about the middle age range, you are really talking about programs that would go on between four-thirty and six in the afternoon. CBS is not on the air at that time because that time period belongs to the local stations."

The current network practice of going off the air in the late afternoons is not deeply rooted in precedent; many of us can remember afternoon shows like *Howdy Doody* and the *Mickey Mouse Club*.

"Mr. Dann, suppose the feeling becomes general that the local stations are not serving kids properly. Would CBS ever reconsider taking to the air in the afternoon to fill the vacuum?"

"Absolutely," replied Mike Dann.

Then I asked the network official to tell me which of his programs he considered showcase.

"Certainly, *Captain Kangaroo*—and then we also offer the *CBS Children's Festival* and the *CBS Children's Hour*."

Mike Dann was especially ecstatic about CBS's latest *Children's Hour* venture, a dramatic series which he explained goes "at noon, right smack at the height of the cartoon block," providing a sixty-minute unanimated stretch. Unfortunately, there are only three of these dramatic shows throughout the entire year. While it is admittedly only a minor point, noon in the East is not precisely the apex of the children's viewing period. Nielsen figures show a drop-off between 11:00 A.M. and 12:00 P.M. on Saturdays of nearly a million child viewers. While the *Children's Hour* does seem to some to represent something of a breakthrough for CBS, television critic Jack Gould remains unconvinced of the network's real intent.

"It's well to keep in mind," Gould said, "that these one-shot, two-shot, or three-shot deals don't really represent the network's basic schedule at all. They're put on in a cluster —frequently around holidays, a lot of noise is made about them, and it's all to create the impression that things are looking up. You can't convince me that with the high ratings CBS has had this year (1969–1970) that they're about to change a blessed thing."

Mike Dann's prediction that the *Film Festival* would continue in its fourth season (1969–1970) turned into something of a flick-flicker. The series, which had had universal appeal among children and adults in previous years, had been presented with regularity on Sunday afternoons. Suddenly it dissipated into one or two films being shown because the network said it had run out of fresh films. Why the delightful films of previous seasons were not shown again remained a mystery. It is quite all right to repeat the *Charlie Brown* series, we are informed, because kids love repetition. Yet it is not cricket to repeat good *films* because, we're told this time, kids do not go in for repetition. This is a clear example of the occult reasoning power of network logic, a process on which CBS assuredly has no monopoly. It overlooks the fact that new young audiences come along every year; for these kids the films would be as new as ever. Meantime, CBS said it would go on looking for "really new films for the 1970–1971 season," and we are left with little to do except stamp our feet and shout for the lady up front to kindly remove her hat.

I wrapped up my interview with Dann with two questions. "Who are the people who advise you in programming matters?"

With a thoughtful look in his CBS eye, Mr. Dann ducked briefly behind a hedge and answered, "Everybody."

"And who makes the final decisions, sir, on programs at CBS?"

Gathering some papers into a neat pile, Dann replied, "When it comes to that, I'm the one who makes program recommendations to CBS management."

Mike Dann fully appreciated the opportunities afforded him by CBS and in fact was one of the highest salaried officials at the network. But in private life he was haunted by the directions in which commercial television appeared headed. His concern for quality, sometimes at the expense of rating numbers, produced a raspy relationship with Robert Wood, who had become the new president of the CBS network. Our conversation took place in December 1969. In mid-June 1970 Dann resigned from CBS to accept the position of vice president of the Children's Television Workshop. Mr. Dann's resources are now directed at promoting CTW's *Sesame Street* on a global scale with foreign language versions of the public television program.

The Better Part of Valor

The National Broadcasting Company has always been famous for its guided tours; they have gone on since the 1930's. So it is not surprising that when a reporter comes to interview a top official there he may find himself escorted into the executive's office by a press relations man who hangs about to answer questions the executive may experience difficulty handling alone.

Larry White is NBC's East Coast vice president in charge of programming. The responsibility for children's fare is ultimately his. White has a well-groomed look about him and he bears a slight resemblance to the late Hollywood actor Jack Carson. The NBC official said he had not come to this post by mounting the rungs of the sales ladder; that he had always considered himself a program man.

White views the medium of television as a big chunk of today's culture. Does he believe TV has a high degree of credibility, that reality and fantasy can at times be confused?

"I think," White replied, "you have to divide entertainment from nonentertainment programs. I think people will be credible about news, documentary statement of fact on TV. But when you're talking about entertainment programs, I do not have that kind of contempt for the American public. I still believe they know it's a story. Why, the littlest kids know it's a story and the bad guy is going to get caught by the good guy. It's not real — it's a fake. You can't convince me it's happening in an entertainment concept. I just don't agree with that."

"Mr. White, some people have suggested that cartoons pander to the worst taste in kids. Do you agree?"

"Who says that?"

"Parents, mainly."

"I don't think parents say that. I think professional TV critics say that."

The press relations official allowed that cartoons are a *form,* that there are such things as good and bad cartoons and that watching NBC would show how good some cartoons can be.

"When you have to choose between a show that will probably bring high ratings and one that is a quality show but isn't likely to do as well, how do you make such a difficult decision?"

"You deal with it in the most intelligent manner you can.

Aware that you're trying to do the best things you can. But aware also that you're part of a business operation."

"Can this be embarrassing at times for you?"

"No. If I were embarrassed I would get out of the business and sell shoes."

The press relations official told us that NBC lavishes a tremendous amount of money on its children's shows and that the network does not permit financial considerations to stand in the way of quality programs. He pointed to *H. R. Pufnstuf* and said in that one show alone the network is pouring "a ridiculous amount of money."

We asked Mr. White to tell us about his showcase programs, and he talked at great length about the Saturday block. Would NBC consider programming for children in the afternoons if the network considered that local stations were not doing an adequate job for the kids?

"If we were to do that," replied White, "a lot of people might say: 'How dare they lock the kids up for another two-and-a-half hours?' Let the kids go out and play, and let them do their homework. And let them have a learning experience. I don't think it is incumbent on us to provide a service that is specific in these terms. I just don't believe it."

Evolution of Pacification?

Shortly after these interviews took place there was a strange bubbling activity at the three networks. It seems to have coincided with the disclosure of Nielsen figures indicating that National Educational Television's *Sesame Street* had very high ratings. The program was proving that even quality shows can have high numbers. NBC was the first to make a startling announcement in January 1970.

NBC president Julian Goodman picked public affairs director George Heinemann to hold a historic new post, vice president of children's programs. The Heinemann appointment appeared to herald a new era for young people's television. Up to that point, no network had even conceived of granting such importance to programming for children. Heinemann's promotion gave rise for hope, yet there were a few disturbing signs that the new vice presidency might be simply a token gesture. Television critic Jack Gould pointed out that the announcement (supposedly one of great significance) was made in a speech by Mr. Goodman in far-off Omaha, Nebraska. The trumpets could not, he said, be heard in New York at all. Then there was the rather cryptic comment by Mr. Goodman that we should not expect big things to happen right away. And still more disturbing was the statement that Mr. Heinemann would report not to top NBC management but to senior vice president White. Although NBC would have us accept its pledge that Heinemann will be given the latitude he needs and deserves, skeptics say the corporate structural arrangement sounds as though the Heinemann post comes equipped with a hidden tether.

Chances are excellent that if you enter George Heinemann's office you will not find him sitting behind a desk. You would be lucky even to find a desk in his room at all. He regards a desk as a kind of trap, preferring instead a schoolroom-like bench or an old leather chair and typewriter table. His papers are never scattered about, but are generally in a neat pile on the floor or in a nearby closet. That might drive a somewhat more orthodox executive straight up the wall. The man himself has the shining face of a schoolboy; one might go so far as to describe him as a living Hummel figure. His manner is blunt and he is not famous for beating around bushes. While Heinemann is normally soft-spoken, he can also raise his voice in anger sufficiently to make a driving wind stand still out of respect. George Heinemann's approaches to life, to people, and to his own work have at times been so bold that more than a few have come away perhaps questioning his sanity. But that is because such honesty and such a childlike quality in a grown man seem irreconcilable.

The originator of such outstanding programs as *Ding Dong School, Animal Kingdom* (once called *Zoo Parade*), and the *NBC Children's Theatre* has succeeded in holding on to a giant portion of his childhood imagination. He says, "It's those few people who retain that imagination who end up the creative contributors in the adult world. And they are always looked up to by the rest of the adults as being nuts, crazy, goofy or strange."

Few people in commercial television are more qualified than George Heinemann to run a children's programming division. Probably nobody in TV knows kids better or cares more about them. Listen to some of his ideas:

"I insist on treating the child as an adult within his framework and on his level. I won't talk down my nose to them. And most particularly, I will not do programs that *I* think are cute or great for him. What I *will* do are the programs *he* really enjoys, the kind of programs he wants to participate in. The philosophy behind the *NBC Children's Theatre* series is to have the parent and child share an experience together. Most programs are baby-sitters for kids. Now, I try hard to have name stars on shows for one reason

— so that the parent will sit down and share the experience with the child. That way, the child will have somebody to communicate with *after the show is over,* which is the richness of storytelling — forgotten in this age of video."

On the program void for the middle range children:

"The child in the middle range is *not* being provided for [by the commercial networks on a regular basis]. Everybody now is satisfying the very young child. They weren't doing that two or three years ago. I'm doing my own surveys now. If I find the need for this group is there and not being met properly, I'm going to try to meet it while I'm here."

Heinemann on the qualities of a good children's programmer:

"The nice thing to be able to do [in this position] is to think like a child. And it's hard to think like a child. If you have that ability, the child knows it instantly."

The new vice president on children's programming:

"The child is a total person within himself. The evil is the adult who programs for the child because he programs what *he* thinks the child wants to have, but doesn't take the time to find out what the *child* really wants. There is this idea that we must not spoil our youth. We must not get at the little children, we must not hurt the innocent children. Well, we live in a kind of two-way world. On one hand, it's perfectly all right for us to do all kinds of horrendous things but it's not all right for the child to know about them or do those things. We just go about convincing ourselves that we're protecting the innocent. But the innocent, in my opinion, are the adults. *They* are the ones who do not know what the world is all about. They are busy distorting and over-protecting their kids."

And George Heinemann offers a refreshing view of network obligations:

"Our responsibility is to find out what is needed by the people. We operate on the airways owned by the people, that is true. But, at the same time, we must get out, survey the national areas, and I'm beginning to do that now. I don't think a network should operate unless it can do better programs than local stations can offer — and the networks *must* peak the national problems. When it comes to children, here is one of my big postulates: for a child, entertainment is often education. For a child, learning something can be entertainment. In our adult minds we divorce entertainment from education, but the child is perfectly willing to accept it. So, therefore, we should introduce into our programming entertainment features that encompass life experiences and real things. That's the kind of thing that will appeal to a broad enough group of people to offer a daily children's program. And we will have it someday if there is a need for it. I'm going to try to find that need."

It is to be hoped the appointment of George Heinemann to oversee the full range of programming for young people at NBC represents not a corporate maneuver to placate the public but a genuine desire on the part of NBC to upgrade the complete profile of television for the children's audience.

A few weeks after the NBC move, CBS and ABC let it be known they were making changes in the children's program area. CBS named Allen Ducovny, a former vice president for

TV at the Nashville Periodical Company, publishers of comic books, to be director of children's programs at the network. Ducovny, the CBS release announced, will report to a new daytime program chief, Fred Silverman. So, while the executive announcement sounds impressive, the shift puts the children's executive not two steps from the top but three.

ABC appointed Charles Martin Jones, a former MGM animationist and producer, to be executive director of children's programs. Mr. Jones, a coauthor of Bugs Bunny cartoons, has promised to bring to kids programs that "educate as well as entertain." Mr. Jones, says ABC, will report to programer Marshall Karp, so autonomy in this case can hardly be expected.

If the latter announcements were meant to create ground-thundering tremors, they failed. They did not even appear in the local New York newspapers, but were printed only in the television trade journals.

4 AND A LITTLE CHILD SHALL LEAD THEM

The precise economic impact of children's programs on the total economic picture of television is difficult to assess properly. There are the glowing accounts in magazines that trumpet huge profits. And there are the officials in television — some boastful, others reserved, often tight-lipped — who do little to shed light on the guarded ledgers. Ask a network man if his company is using black or red ink in the children's column and he will avoid the question by quoting rating figures. These, of course, bolster his view that kids are watching but really tell you nothing about whether the network is making money, losing money, or breaking even. We have to remember that big gross billings do not necessarily mean big net profits. There are the huge cost factors to be subtracted. It is true that in the highly competitive struggles, high ratings sometimes allow a network sales department to raise its advertising charges, and, provided cost figures are held constant, high profit margins will result. But cost figures do not always remain constant. On the other hand, lower ratings can force a network's costs up in the competitive push to find a more powerful audience grabber, and its profit margin gets squeezed even tighter.

It is impossible to come up with precise figures to show typical costs and profits of programs, but we have made a valiant effort to arrive at some fairly accurate guesstimates. To do this, we resorted to wearing a pair of gumshoes, a trenchcoat, and finding an assortment of undercover men at the networks and advertising agencies whose sole price was the promise of anonymity. And it also meant the checking of a myriad of details gathered here and there, conversations with television executives, and the time-consuming process of cross-checking to isolate many rumors from facts and truths from half-truths.

The Economics of Cartoon Shows

Cartoons comprise the backbone of Saturday morning fare for the three major networks, just as they do for many local stations around the country throughout much of the entire week. At NBC we asked vice president Larry White to assess *Business Week*'s statement ("TV's Saturday Goldmine," August 2, 1969) that all three networks were realizing $20 million in profits from the Saturday strip alone. White replied it sounded high to him. A reliable source from within CBS, however, confirmed the figure with this important reservation. He said the figure of $20 million was a fairly accurate accounting of *gross profits,* which *Business Week* had neglected to report.

There have been other figures floating around that require some explanation. For example, another publication reported that combined major network revenues from the cartoons had come to $90 million a year. To people who have difficulty trying to decipher the intricate accounting jargon, it all sounds very confusing. Yet deep down there is the visceral feeling that the networks are really cleaning up.

The fact is that everybody has grossly overstated sales and profits from the Saturday shows.

Revenue figures are the dollars taken in by the network from advertising sources — in other words, total sales. From the revenue are subtracted operating, administrative, and talent costs. This results in a *gross profit* figure. These are the two figures often given or leaked to the press, but they really are not meaningful until you arrive at the *net profit* figure. Net profit figures are arrived at after subtracting from gross profit such items as taxes, retained earnings and depreciation costs. And it is this net profit figure that becomes highly classified information.

Nobody can tell you outright what the cost of a typical cartoon half-hour show runs because so much of the cost differential depends on such things as artwork and cinematic effect. We asked NBC's Larry White to give us a rough idea, and he responded that he would judge a good practical range would be $50,000 to $75,000 per half hour. Up to a point, Mr. White was correct, but he forgot to mention that you have to divide his figures by *six*. The reason is that the networks obtain a license to show a cartoon, but are allowed six reruns over a period of two years. This more accurately puts the cost of a typical cartoon show at somewhere between $8,000 and $10,000 a week. The costs can be dropped even lower if a network will tolerate more limited animation effects. Most of ABC's cartoons use *very* limited animation, an indication they are paying a good deal less to the cartoon makers. So it is possible to bring the half hour cost down to perhaps $6,000 in some instances. It all depends on how tight your budget is and just how much poor artwork the programmer is willing to compromise on.

Now we arrive at the question implied earlier: are the networks actually making a haul on the Saturday cartoons? The rule seems to be that if the kids get hung up on one cartoon series, they will generally stay all morning with the channel on which it appears. In 1969–1970 CBS was the favorite channel, and as a result the network attracted more than half of the available children's audience. This meant that their *gross profits* alone exceeded $10 million, and our CBS source told us they were "definitely doing very well" in the net profit department. But what of the two rival networks? NBC and ABC were splitting the remaining audience and not doing "that well." NBC's Larry White, in expressing his disappointment at NBC's failure to take the lead, commented, "Our biggest victory in this area is to break even." He went on to add, "Here, in the program department, we operate thankfully divorced from the profit and loss statement. We don't ask anything about it and aren't told." Strange words from the head of programming division of the National Broadcasting Company.

But is it actually possible to hope merely to break even under present circumstances? Our CBS source says it *is* possible, but highly unlikely. In the past CBS has run on a break-even course and has even lost money at times. But our man there says that in today's market, when advertisers are lining up to get on Saturday cartoon shows, the likelihood is that all three networks are making money. Our review of ABC's Saturday strip, though, shows a dearth of commercial material and substitution of public service announcements. The suggestion is not that ABC has suddenly gone soft on the kids and done away with commercials, but that the ineup of advertisers is perhaps outside Blackrock or the RCA building, and decidedly not in front of the ABC skyscraper. So it would not seem unreasonable to suspect that ABC is operating bravely at a loss.

Ledger de main

The country's only daily program for children carried by a commercial network is the long-established *Captain Kangaroo* hour. There has been a good deal of speculation that this highly creative program represents a cost drain to CBS. Cost figures have been put at between $45,000 and $50,000 a week, all of which means it costs about the same as a typical cartoon program. *Captain Kangaroo* is *not* operating at a loss. While it is not producing a big profit, it is, nevertheless, definitely in the profit column.

In general, live children's specials are very costly. A program in the category of the *CBS Children's Hour* probably costs between $200,000 and $300,000 in its entirety. An extravaganza such as NBC's *Peter Pan* originally was produced for around $300,000, but to reproduce that same show today would cost more nearly $600,000. Moreover, these shows are expensive to replay, and when you ask why certain live-action dramas are not repeated more often, you will have to point to the cost figures. The reason is that to rerun a taped live show the network has to pay over half of the original costs for rights and residuals to the performers. These cost factors are spelled out clearly in union contracts.

Programs representative of mixed live and animated effects are NBC's *Banana Splits* and *H. R. Pufnstuf*. Advertising sources have put a production price tag of somewhere in the neighborhood of $156,000 for this kind of program.

If a local station is fortunate enough to find a talente performer who can produce and write a show at the sam time, cost figures can drop unbelievably. To illustrate: i New York, Metromedia's formerly syndicated *Pixanne* show which was seen six days a week, ran probably under $3,00 a program because Jane Norman was both creator an performer.

NET's *Misterogers* program is produced at extremely lo figures only because its originator, Fred Rogers, happens t be so talented. He co-produces the show, writes it and play most of the parts, including creating most of the voices of th puppets. For $300,000 he was able to produce one hundre thirty shows in black and white. And for a time, when h converted to color, he could turn out sixty-five shows for tha sum. Rogers's budget has now gone up slightly becaus material costs keep going up and also because his progra is getting wider distribution throughout the country.

A Word About Advertising Costs

The price of advertised merchandise is certainly ver much a part of television economics. Parents continuall complain about the high costs of TV advertised product particularly toys. While it is true that technology can a count for some of the high prices, another factor is th advertiser's budget. Duncan Farr, the merchandising ma ager for Fisher Price, says, "When you start budgeting ful ten to fifteen per cent of your sales dollar for TV adve tising, you've got to take it out of something. And th something is quality. We put our money, in the main, in the toy, and we've never had anywhere near ten per ce of our sales dollar allotted for advertising. Apparently, th competing larger toy firms like Hasbro, Mattel, and Remco do put that kind of money in it."

From what we have been able to determine, the big toy people are currently budgeting for advertising sums in the neighborhood of between $15 million and $16 million a year. And that helps to explain why the consumer is shelling out so much around Christmas time and why the toys often do not last beyond New Year's morning.

5 ANATOMY OF A MESSAGE

To the strains of the inane lyrics "Catch that pigeon— catch that pigeon," *Dastardly and Muttley* chase through the clouds in their flying machine. Suddenly forgetting about their prey, they turn to the kids in the audience and proceed to sell them another kind of sugar-coated Kellogg's cereal Then the pursuit continues. If you happen to be a very small child, chances are the sales message very much appears to be part of the story adventure.

Later on, the kids are thoroughly absorbed in the trials of the *Flintstones*. Fred Flintstone and his alter ego, Barney Rubble, are bumping along in their custom Flintmobile and finally decide to stop, so they pull over to the shoulder of the road. Both cartoon characters emerge from the car and begin walking away. Then Fred and Barney suddenly wheel about (or so it appears) and begin a direct sales pitch for "deliciously flavored Flintstone vitamins." Are many of the kids aware that the vitamin portion of the TV sequence is *not* part of the story line? The advertisers hope not, because a deliberate advantage is being taken of children who cannot tell where the story line drops off and the commercial line begins. This is a cinematic technique being more and more widely accepted in television advertising and promotion. It calls for the elimination of an accepted film convention, the *fade-to-black,* which signals the end of a total or portion of a story. When the picture goes to black, we have a sense of partial or total finality and know that a fresh idea is about to appear on the screen. In the examples cited above, the TV director makes a *direct cut* or an instantaneous change of scene without resorting to a transition; so we see no fades and no dissolves which would orient us to a new scene of action. The subtle cartoon deception is accomplished by matching the last frame of the story film to the first film frame of the commercial. So just as the last frame of the cartoon in the story comes up on the studio TV monitor, the TV director makes a direct cut to the matching cartoon character in the commercial or public service announcement. The absence of the traditional fade-to-black blurs the boundary between the fantasy of the story and the reality of the product commercial. This procedure can be carried out adroitly enough to confuse even adults. Our quarrel here is not with the commercial, free enterprise system but with the advertisers and broadcasters who resort to unfair psychological manipulation of young people—children who lack the experience to make rational judgments or whose developmental stage does not yet allow for clear distinctions between fantasy and reality.

Although the advertisers and network officials we spoke to denied that "the mice" are frequently subjected to deceptive commercials on television, a look at the screen can refute their denials. The racing cars on television streak by as though jet-propelled, or at least battery-operated. But kids soon discover at home that there are no batteries and that the streak is weak. And little girls who covet all those precocious television dolls quickly learn that the real dolls are poorly constructed and a good deal less proficient at their tasks than they appear to be on the tube. Four-year-old Pamela is a very warm child who loves to play the role of mother. You rarely see her walking around when she is not hugging her Raggedy Ann or one of her soft rubber dolls. For Christmas her parents got her the Baby-Grow-a-Tooth doll they saw advertised on TV. Within the space of only a few days the parents reported the child had lost interest in the doll because "it was not huggable, and just how many times can you watch a tooth grow?"

One major television advertiser remarked that plenty of misconceptions appear on the screen. The FCC, he said, has jumped on a few people who engage in the practice. "These people, who try to see just how far they can go before a whistle is blown, merely back away for a time and wait until the heat is off; then they're right back doing the same things — creating false illusions in ads for the kids." Questionable or subliminal values can be carried with the product message. Such piggybacking techniques take advantage of the fact that people (particularly small kids) are deluded by irrational emotional appeals. Take the television ad for Kool-Aid. Here we see a forlorn boy sitting around when who should hop by but Bugs Bunny. "What's up, Doc — no friends?" Good old Bugs helps stir up some Kool-Aid, and the slogan song "Make Friends with Kool-Aid" fills the air. Presto! The lonely kid is surrounded by an army of little people. Alone, the child is a failure; but throw a product into the picture and he becomes an instant success. It is an idea that television impresses on children when they are still in the crib. And there are a lot of kids who come to believe their social success can be measured in terms of material acquisition.

Children are continually sold fads and useless toys because the advertiser knows perfectly well tiny kids are impractical, open to suggestion, and fickle. Evidence of this fact can be found in the playroom of just about any household where children have grown up. The plastic airplane models that flew but once, the bugles that blew perhaps a couple of times, the little girl's footsies that have never been worn. Hard sell and repetition are the usual techniques of moving fad merchandise, but such oversell can backfire, drawing irritation from parents and children alike. Our own survey showed that most parental resentment toward commercials is directed at these hard pitches; they feel angered by both the high price and the flimsiness of television-advertised toys. Many times a perfectly good toy is not purchased by a TV parent because of the oversell employed.

The people who tell you that television represents a reflection of our times are presenting a rather simplistic view. Television, in large measure, does mirror the culture, but at the same time the medium acts as a prod, speeding up cultural dynamics. And while it may be perfectly true that television exerts but a single influence on our way of life, its voice nevertheless remains shrill and unrelenting. We hear many parents saying with pride that television has matured their youngsters earlier, that no previous generation has been so knowledgeable and sophisticated. One is moved to ask whether maturity is being confused with precociousness. Without a doubt, today's young generation is more product-oriented than any previous one. The exposure that children now have (mainly through TV) to constant explosions of materialistic values must have some drastic impact on their thinking. Surely one is that television is aiding in dwarfing childhood. Children are encouraged to go to things beyond their years. Young girls wear lipstick before they are kissable and training bras long before they reach puberty. Barbie dolls and toy racing cars are teaching kids that true happiness means acquiring a host of accessories. These are some of the values we are allowing to slip into the living room.

The Performer Who Sells

One of the economic facts of life in children's TV is that performers are generally expected to sell products. Many who would prefer not endorsing products are compelled to compromise and make the most of a situation they feel they cannot change. Robert Keeshan (*Captain Kangaroo*, CBS), for instance, refuses to advertise products he finds objectionable or unsuitable for children, and he never permits toys he considers of a violent nature to be sold. Moreover, Keeshan insists on screening all filmed commercials before they hit the air. That is how he makes his peace with the economic necessities of commercial TV. However, most performers ride the crest of the selling waves because they feel they lack the stature or political position to "buck the system." Bob McAllister (*Wonderama*, Metromedia) tells us, "The name of the game is selling. You have to sell spots on the show or you won't be on the air very long. Unfortunately, there is a great deal of garbage sold to kids. There are some very good things that are sold, but I would have to say the bad things outweigh the good. There's no doubt about it."

The testimonial has been a tried and effective sales instrument for years. But critics are now targeting in on testimonials directed to children. They argue that adults have no difficulty distinguishing between the product message and the emotional appeal but that children do. If the performer is successful, he has built up a rapport and relationship with the children over a long period of time. They trust him and they put their confidence in whatever he happens to tell them. Naturally, the products he endorses are met with ready acceptance by young people. Many observers feel that this type of salesmanship is unfair and unethical. An alternative suggested is that performers be prohibited from delivering messages, that commercials be given by a neutral announcer with whom the children do not identify.

Did You Get the Secret Message?

A number of children's programs have come under attack because they amount to giant giveaways and become simply one long train of commercials. On the syndicated *Bozo* show and on Metromedia's *Wonderama,* to illustrate the point, the happy screaming kids are happy because they are making off with an armful of toys. But they never get away before the program MC manages to mention the name of the toy sponsor or potential new sponsor at least once. In between the program segments, the producers inject several commercials honestly labeled as such. It is a unique kind of integration, and the gamble is that the FCC is looking the other way.

Advertising with Children in Mind

A number of TV advertisers merit citation for enlightened approaches to selling, approaches which are firmly anchored in social responsibility. They avoid traditional advertising appeals which depend largely on emotional or value stratagems. Some of these, like the Fisher Price Toy Company, avoid direct selling to children at all. They use straightforward advertising messages to parents and place their commercials on adult programs only. Their messages are clear, straightforward, in excellent taste and devoid of deception. The Healthtex Corporation, a participating sponsor of the *CBS Children's Hour,* realizes that to appeal to children all you need is a simple story line, sometimes humorous, sometimes not. Their commercials contain information about subjects that arouse a child's interest. For instance, why are some people dark and others light? A simple explanation is offered followed by a brief statement about their product. The Xerox Corporation supports outstanding television programs for young people, using good taste in its advertising. Xerox feels a debt of gratitude to television for aiding in the company's rapid growth, and its officials say they want to repay the medium by helping to improve the quality of programming. Accordingly, they operate on a basic philosophy, one element of which is that every program they sponsor must have "an over-purpose that will not only entertain . . . but will tend to stretch the mind, to inspire, to stir the conscience and will require thought." Xerox has moved strongly into the educational publishing business, and the company's advertising appeal is directed to parents and teachers.

The Gulf Oil Corporation has heavily backed television programs on space. Although there is no direct selling appeal to children, their presence in the audience is always borne in mind. Gulf, too, has on occasion supported an outstanding television program for an audience comprised for the most part of young people.

Who among us, no matter what our age, has not been delighted by the brief, enjoyable visits by the Jolly Green Giant between portions of NBC's *Children's Theatre!* Green Giant Foods has repeatedly demonstrated its philosophy of social responsibility to children.

Saturday mornings, and all through the week, the air is filled with the mention of Kellogg cereals. Certainly the company has poured enough money into the medium to reap a rich return on its advertising dollar. But aside from buying some spot ads on *Captain Kangaroo* Kellogg does little to support quality children's programming. The impression I get is that the company is less concerned about what the child will bring away from the set than what the Kellogg company will bring back in dollars and cents.

In sharp contrast to Kellogg's advertising philosophy is that of the Quaker Oats Company. Says Quaker Oats president Robert Stuart, "I think we can always do better. We are concerned that television does potentially have such an influence on kids, that we [at Quaker Oats] have the responsibility to attempt to upgrade the level of programs." To demonstrate that his company means what it says, Stuart said Quaker Oats is picking up a portion of the bill to pay the costs for showing *Sesame Street* in Chicago and Buffalo. Perhaps what is more astounding is the fact that Quaker Oats will be competing directly against itself, since *Sesame*

Street plays opposite Quaker Oats–sponsored programs on commercial television outlets. "Our big hope," says Robert Stuart, "is that we can show there are good listening audiences (watching *Sesame Street*) and that kids watch this . . . that there's an audience out there benefiting from the program. From this, we are hopeful it will stimulate the producers of commercial children's television to improve the quality of their output."

Telecasting Standards and Practices

Over the years the idea that the printed page is "infallible" has taken hold with large segments of the reading audience. Now there is a tendency to include electronic "pages," with the result that there are some people who think of what they view on television as infallible. This being the case, ways must be found to protect portions of the population against harmful, misleading or illegal information. At the major networks, whole departments have been set up to deal with the problem of maintaining the integrity of the public airways. These departments of standards and practices amount to commercial message filtration plants, and their prime function is to scrutinize all commercials prior to air to make sure they contain no false, deleterious, unlawful information. That task is difficult enough, considering the voluminous amount of material that has to be examined, some of it dependent on the fragilities of subjective decision. But, in addition, standards and practices departments are frequently faced with making value judgments and deciding questions of taste, matters falling quite openly in the arena of subjective opinion. It is these matters of value and taste that have drawn the heaviest fire from critical circles. The conflict between what constitutes censorship and what remains freedom of expression is far from being resolved.

At the local station level, standards and practices of operation are too diverse to attempt to describe here. Suffice it to say that usually the supervisory role is assumed by one or more members of the management team. But there are still many stations where no such supervision takes place at all. Often when there appears to be an equal balance in a question of judgment the weight of economics will become the determining factor. (The economic factor inevitably plays a part at the networks, too, despite the fact that the machinery for supervision is more intricate.) The program manager of one major metropolitan station, who was formerly a network official, describing the problems presented at his station said, "We are relatively hamstrung in these matters because unless a commercial is deceptive or illegal there is little we can do about it. I certainly agree that many commercials we use are totally obnoxious."

Even at the circus sideshows, the patent medicine men knew kids were not fair game. Tonics to grow hair abounded along with liniment for lumbago, but vendors knew better than to aim their medical wonders at kids. Now the pharmaceutical houses have discovered the financial potential of the children's TV audience, and the airways are replete with deliciously flavored vitamin pills. This shift of direct sell of medical products to children is filled with hazards. What is to prevent the child, entranced with the marvelous flavor of vitamins, from trying sugar-coated aspirin or other more potent drugs? Are we broadcasters any less guilty in permitting the airways to be used in this way? If program standards and practices departments do not draw these lines, who will?

New York Mayor John Lindsay grappled with this problem when he told a convention of city school principals in a February 1970 speech that television advertising is propelling children toward drug addiction even before they reach school age. "The schools," he said as quoted in the *New York Times* of February 7, 1970, "are failing to counter the advertising propaganda about the virtues of drugs and are becoming the training grounds for the next generation of addicts." Mayor Lindsay continued, "A child will see eight thousand hours of television before he enrolls in school and what has he been taught? To relax minor tensions with a pill, to take off weight with a pill, to win status and sophistication with a cigarette, to wake up and be happy, relieve tensions with pills." The mayor said effective warnings should be issued against the indiscriminate use of pills to a generation that is turning more and more to drugs as a solution to its problems.

The major networks and the majority of television stations subscribe to the National Association of Broadcasters Television Code. Subscribers pledge to limit the number and duration of commercials presented during any given part of the day or evening. It should be stressed that these restrictions do not carry the force of the law; they represent only pledges that the station or network will adhere to the NAB's ethical broadcasting standards embodied in the code. The outer limits of the code, though, are quite elastic, and individual station or network policies are permitted to push hard against those code limits. To illustrate the point, the networks are urged to comply with a maximum of three minutes per half hour of commercial time in the evenings. In the daytime, commercial time can go to five or six minutes a half hour. Our own check in January and February 1970 found the networks complying with this commercial schedule. But just prior to Christmas our count showed the Saturday morning commercial count up to seven minutes per half hour on the average for all three networks. And in September 1969, ACT (Action for Children's Television, a group described in chapter 17) clocked fifty minutes and thirty seconds of commercial time during the three-hour Saturday morning cartoon run, about eight minutes a half hour. While these seasonal variations appear to stretch the code limits, NAB officials explain this is allowable. They say the individual station or network policy can exceed the recommended NAB Code restrictions *provided they are within what are called the code's "outermost limits."* These latter curbs permit the use of ten minutes of nonprogram material per half hour in prime time and sixteen minutes of nonprogram material per half hour in nonprime time. The NAB defines "nonprogram" material as commercials, program billboards, and program credits that exceed thirty seconds. In checking to see if the proper name of the code is the "code of good practices," the NAB said it is now encouraging stations to drop the words "good practices."

Some people have urged the networks to consider following a European custom of lumping commercials at the beginning or end of a program to offer more separation between the program content and the commercial portion of the program. NBC considers the suggestion impractical; CBS says the idea may be worth trying.

The suggestion that the economic and moral conflicts of commercial television can be resolved by strict new federal regulations or government watchdog committees is completely impracticable. No room for such machinery can or should exist within our free enterprise system. Admittedly, broadcasting's self-policing practices have been lax in many instances. We have seen evidence of this in the handling of children's television. One reason for the laxity is that often those concerned with enforcing such practices are not sufficiently informed about the potential effects their decisions may bring about. Another is that the temptations offered by the opportunity for profit may be difficult to reject. Yet when the choice is one between the introduction of questionable values to an impressionable, young audience and that of economic advantage, the latter must yield. The fact that parents must accept the responsibility of teaching their children acceptable values and standards does not relieve the broadcasters of their equal responsibility of seeing to it that children are not exploited.

6 PUBLIC TELEVISION AND THE FOURTH NETWORK

While the system of noncommercial television in this country has been with us for some time, its sudden expansion and changes have been so swift that precisely what it is all about remains a mystery to some and a confusion to others.

Unfortunately, the very term *educational TV* (ETV), as noncommercial television is more commonly known, often conjures up the somber vision of a formal classroom setting. Quite a few people envision it as a video trip to the public library. One parent told us she would not let her child watch an education channel because five days a week behind a school bench is certainly enough. Another mother reported her daughter enjoyed all the fine programs ETV had to offer, citing as examples such commercial programs as *Romper Room, I Love Lucy* and *The Brady Bunch.*

Public Television

Educational television channels are owned by educational institutions or by other nonprofit groups. All of them have in common the fact that their programs are not supported by advertising revenue. Unless the television channel is operated on "closed circuit" at a college campus or unless the TV channel produces a very feeble signal, the picture output can be picked up on the home screen.

Programming appearing on an educational TV station may be one of two general kinds. *Instructional* TV is directed at students in the classroom. These programs are of the formal educational variety, for the most part, and are the sort of programs some think of when the term educational TV crops up in conversation. The second general kind of programming beamed by ETV is called *public television.* Public TV encompasses just about anything of human interest and importance which at the moment the commercial broadcasters are not ready or willing to support by advertising. The topics can be more exciting, more controversial, and every bit as entertaining as programs on commercial television channels. These are definitely not video trips to the public library; their funding comes from public and nonprofit sources as well as from individual donation. Public television has the added advantage of not having to cater to large masses of the viewing audience, which enables this kind of television to offer more controversial, sometimes more esoteric programming.

The Emergence of the Fourth Network (PBS)

In 1968, following the suggestion of the Carnegie Commission on Educational Television, the Congress established the Corporation for Public Broadcasting. Its purpose is to receive and disburse governmental and private funds to extend and improve public television programming. In effect, the Corporation for Public Broadcasting became the real parent of public telecasting. Even as late as into the Seventies much of the funding for public TV had been coming from the Ford and Carnegie foundations. Now, with the CPB in the picture, the private foundations' funding was gradually to be phased out. If the foundations still wanted to support part of the public TV funding, provision for that was made.

In March 1970, CPB created the new Public Broadcasting Service (PBS), which from that point on became an actual fourth national TV network. Prior to this time, a nonprofit programming unit called National Educational Television (NET) functioned as a quasi network. But NET lacked the true status of a television network. It had no regular electronically interconnected stations and no production facilities of its own. Primarily, NET contracted with independent producers to supply individual programs, which were then reproduced by NET in Ann Arbor, Michigan, and distributed to member stations by mail. Many of NET's productions were carried out by local educational TV stations around the country that had production facilities such as those in Boston, Pittsburgh, and New York.

The new fourth network, PBS, does not produce any of the programs. It will contract for new programs produced elsewhere and coordinate the distribution in place of NET. That distribution by 1971 is to be totally via electronic interconnection. In other words, stations will be part of the PBS network, joined by coaxial cable or microwave linkage to permit simultaneous telecasting to all of the individual stations around the nation. The commercial networks, of course, are all interconnected in this manner; fifty-one points along this electronic network are now in service. By the 1971 target date there are to be in all ninety-six of these major interconnections completed. But in addition there are smaller trunk lines of interconnections in operation now, so that by the time the golden spike is struck on the ninety-sixth station, ninety more channels on trunk lines automatically will join in. That will complete a national fourth electronically interconnected television network for use in public telecasting.

The emergence of an interconnected network raises the question of what has become of NET. As we have suggested, PBS must contract to have TV productions made. NET's function has changed, and it has resurfaced as the major supplier of programs for the PBS network. However, PBS will be supplied programs from other sources as well: the production facilities of state educational networks (Rocky Mountain Educational Network, Eastern Educational Network, Connecticut Educational Television Corporation, etc.), independent producers, and perhaps from foreign sources.

The producers of *Sesame Street,* the Children's Television Workshop, had been a semiautonomous arm of NET during the period the latter functioned as a network. With the structural changes in public broadcasting, NET spun off the workshop as an independent production unit. The workshop, therefore, has come to parallel NET as another program supplier to the PBS network, but it specializes in children's programming. This, to add just a peppering of confusion, does not mean NET will cease producing children's programs of its own. NET is to continue producing both children's and adult educational programming, and, accordingly, has a children's programming division and an adult division.

A Look Backward at NET

Before the Public Broadcasting Service network was established, nearly all of the country's educational channels were affiliated with National Educational Television. NET furnished the educational stations with nearly fifty per cent of their programming needs. It produced or obtained from foreign television sources five or more hours of new TV shows a week. About half of these were cultural productions, the remaining half public affairs presentations. Probably the largest contributor to NET's bank of programs has been the British Broadcasting Corporation. But, in addition, NET supplied its affiliates with one of their major assets, several hours of daily children's TV shows each week, including the popular *Sesame Street, Misterogers' Neighborhood, The Friendly Giant* and *What's New*. Approximately two-thirds of NET productions were performed by NET staff or by independent producers in New York. The remaining third were carried out by affiliated local ETV channels under NET supervision and distributed. The Ford Foundation supplied the bulk of NET's funding and the rest came from government subsidies.

NET's Children's Division

For many years the man who guided the fortunes of NET's Children's Division was a gentle-mannered former Milwaukeean named Paul Taff. Since this interview was completed, PBS came into existence and Taff has become the president of Connecticut's statewide educational TV system, the Connecticut Educational Television Corporation. Taff is confident that at present PBS is the only network truly devoted to children of all ages. The effort has been to follow the policies laid down by NET while Taff was directing children's programming. It is difficult to argue the former NET official's point, because NET had been the only network concerned with meeting the emotional and intellectual needs not only of preschoolers, but of the middle age range children as well. NET's toughest problem, said pipe-smoking Paul Taff, was simply money; working on a fraction of a commercial network budget, NET did a tremendous job.

The limitation of funds at NET meant a good many corners had to be cut in production techniques that affected the overall quality. And that shortage of capital prevented setting up the needed electronic interconnections. Ironically, it was the growing costs of tape duplication and distribution that provided the real impetus for eventual electronic interconnection and helped spell the demise of NET as a quasinetwork. The duplication process generally allowed programs to reach all stations within a two-week period. From a programming standpoint, the distribution lag thwarted NET from putting on shows that were very seasonal or current. Children have become so accustomed to commercial television's timely programs that they soon developed an awareness of the time lag on NET shows. Five-year-old Timmy, for instance, asked his mother why Misterogers never talked about Christmas during the Christmas season. After all, Captain Kangaroo always did on CBS.

Even though NET was heavily committed to serving the needs of young people, the Children's Division, as in the case of the three major commercial networks, had only a director, not an autonomous vice president. The indications are the PBS will not have such an officer either.

One of NET's additional weaknesses as a network was that its audience feedback measurements could best be described as primitive. One had the impression reaction was gauged solely on the basis of the weight of a bundle of letters received at the affiliated ETV stations. Paul Taff admitted he was skeptical of audience measurement techniques but he had the *feeling* NET was picking up a children's audience in the ghetto as well as in the middle-class neighborhoods. Nevertheless, his *belief* (and he stressed that it was only his belief) was that the larger share of NET's audience consisted of the better-educated groups because "they see the value of good TV programs for their children and, therefore, encourage them to watch good TV."

We asked the children's director if he believed the kids watched NET by their own choice or because of parental guidance.

"I think youngsters don't make distinctions between channels," Taff told us. "I think it's the nature of the program . . . the presentation of it. . . . When the program really reaches the child, he'll watch it whether it's on channel two or sixty-eight. It is up to the parent to encourage better screening, better viewing habits." The director blew a reflective puff from his pipe. "Children, when left on their own, are inclined to go for the action packages because they've been conditioned to this. But I think once a child sees Fred Rogers and understands what *Misterogers* does for him . . . in the sense of reaching him, talking directly to him . . . really caring about him . . . then I firmly believe he will turn to Fred Rogers . . . not to an innocuous cartoon."

"Do you think children do much *thinking* with TV, or do you have the impression they're going through a passive activity?" we wanted to know.

"It's not necessarily passive. I suspect this is where the distinction comes between what the majority of programs on commercial TV are doing and the majority of programs on noncommercial TV. It would be our intent that noncommercial TV does *involve* the youngster more . . . while he is watching we feel there is more thinking going on . . . than, say, when he is watching a cartoon. Every program in the *Misterogers* series is designed to continue the thought pattern." Taff said sometimes you look at a child and say to yourself, " 'He's not thinking at all.' " Then he related this story:

"We have a youngster living next door—maybe he's three or three and a half years old. He watches the *Misterogers* program but, according to his mother, he says very little while the program is on. He just sits rather physically passive. He'll talk back to the set when Misterogers says 'Good-bye.' Not so very long ago, I saw the youngster outside and very spontaneously I said, 'Hi, neighbor!' Why, he broke into a big smile and replied, 'I'm Misterogers's neighbor, too!' Now that to me shows an active mental participation. That was part of his thinking . . . a part of his being."

"Mr. Taff, do you think children are introduced to adult facets too quickly?"

"I think so. The child today may know more . . . may have the knowledge . . . but he may have the knowledge without having the wisdom to use that knowledge."

NET has been the only network supplying programs every weekday to the middle range children, those children roughly between six and ten. We asked Paul Taff if they are difficult to program for and why.

"I think this *is* a hard age group to program for. But to me it's perhaps the most fascinating. I've often said that youngsters of this age are interested in almost anything, i it is made understandable to them. You can take any subject from a moonshot to music and kids will be interested. But they don't seem to like strictly studio-produced shows. You really have to go places, to use film, to use remote trucks, and this all costs money." So, as far as Taff was concerned, the big challenge to middle range children's programming was largely a problem of money.

Does Taff believe TV violence is harmful?

"I can only give you my *opinion* on this. I think that watching violence *can* affect children's thinking or their actions, now or in the future. How? Well, by making them indifferent to it. And I feel that the cumulative effect is leaving a big impression."

How does Taff think educational TV can now effectively compete with commercial TV?

"The competition from commercial TV doesn't concern us . . . there isn't any!"

Many parents replying to our survey said there was really little of value on television, especially during the weekday afternoons. We hope they have discovered there are acres of diamonds on the local educational TV channels waiting to be carted away; all that is needed is the willingness to look for them. It is also a good idea to check the ETV channel during the morning hours when many stations are providing in-school television for the classroom. Some of these programs can be fascinating to parents, too, and watching a program the child is viewing in school could provide a basis for helpful discussion when the youngster comes home.

7 WHO'S WATCHING AND WHEN?

In commercial television, probably no word is more often used, more often misused, quoted, feared, respected, and misunderstood than the term *rating*. If so many people directly under the television umbrella fail to come to grips with the term, small wonder much of the general public has come to conceive of a rating as a kind of whimsical hobgoblin that steers the fate of a television program. We hear that programs soar or sink, that it all depends on whether the rating acts as a buoy or an anchor. We have come to accept all of this, yet the mystique about ratings, to a large extent, remains.

The fact that a program may be viewed by a great number of people is not always enough to assure its survival. Often the network or advertiser is not satisfied that those who are watching happen to be the targeted segment of the audience. Demographic composition of the audience may turn out to be the decisive factor. After seventeen years with CBS, the Red Skelton show was dropped in the 1970–1971 season. The Associated Press reported at least one reason was that statistics showed that "42% of his 32 million viewers were fifty years old and over, 34% were between eighteen and forty-nine, and the rest seventeen and under." Almost immediately, rival network NBC signed the comedian up, reportedly because "the Skelton show ranked twenty-ninth in its list of 'demographic appeal to audiences in the eighteen to forty-nine age group' and was number eight in the popularity list."

The A. C. Nielsen Company calls itself the largest market research organization in the world. While other similar firms provide TV audience rating services, certainly the Nielsen TV rating index is among the most familiar, and it is for this reason that we have elected to explain the concept of ratings utilizing the Nielsen methods. In the cases of the other survey firms measurement systems may differ, as will the size of the samplings, but the basic objectives do not vary. The idea is to determine who is watching television and which programs they are watching. One may argue that only those who are at all concerned with commercial TV should be concerned with the rating system. But as noncommercial television attempts more and more to compete against the commercial stations the rating systems are going to have to take on added importance. It is the only effective method of ascertaining how well any one program is holding up against its competition.

Who Uses Audience Research

TV audience research data such as that compiled by Nielsen can prove an invaluable tool to almost anybody with an interest in the medium. This includes programmers and producers, who need to have timely estimates of TV viewing activity; advertisers and their agencies, who are concerned that their products are reaching the desired audience; and broadcast time buyers, who try to match a specific audience with a specific advertiser.

Basically, it may be desirable to have purely general statistics, to know simply how many people are watching TV, or perhaps the profile of the viewers may be more significant. Let us suppose that you, as an advertiser, are attempting to sell a product like toothpaste. If research showed a potential TV show had good drawing power, the composition of the audience would not be vital since the product has universal appeal; so numerical data might suffice for your decision to advertise on that TV program. Now let's suppose you are a station programmer trying to build a show for small children. You can discover from straightforward numerical data that your show has a lot of viewers, but you will still be in the soup until you can determine just who the viewers are. If they are not predominantly small children, you know something is wrong with the show and that changes will have to be made. Clearly it is sometimes vital to have more than general viewing figures, and it may be essential to know the composition of the audience tuned to the program.

The Nielsen Media Research Division is prepared to tell its clients both the estimated size of a TV audience and a good deal about the composition of the audience. Some subscribers, such as the networks, are primarily interested in learning how a given program is doing across the entire country. Nielsen meets this need by furnishing what is called the Nielsen Television Index, or NTI. NTI provides estimates of continental U.S. audiences for *sponsored network television programming*. The phrase is a key one, because unless that network program happens to be sponsored, it will not appear on the Nielsen report.

But regional or local telecasters and advertisers are not

nterested in competition other than that in their own back-
yards. For their needs Nielsen provides a service called Niel-
en Station Index, or NSI. The NSI reports comprise esti-
nates of viewing county-by-county and market-by-market to
tations within the continental U.S. and Hawaii. Included
n each of these individualized market reports are estimates
of audiences for all programming of all of the stations con-
idered "reportable" in each market.

Nielsen considers some stations in the country "unreportable." The concern is that samplings from them are for
ne reason or another not sufficiently reliable. The research
rganization has prescribed certain conditions for stations to
e considered reportable in its samplings, and any station
or which the minimums are not met is not listed in the
eports. A television station may be "unreportable" if it
lects to serve only specialized segments of the mass audi-
nce. Nielsen also will not report stations that may be newly
perational or that are experiencing technical difficulties if
ney are achieving low viewing activity. No matter how care-
ully any sample is drawn and executed it is virtually impos-
ble to eliminate all potential biases, but Nielsen's efforts
re to keep such potential biases as small as possible. The
ajority of noncommercial stations do not appear in the
Nielsen reports. That, says Nielsen, is primarily because
neir programming patterns are highly specialized, and
nerefore, reach audiences too small to measure, not because
ne stations happen to be noncommercial.

Inasmuch as Nielsen is faced with measuring the viewing
abits of unfathomable man, the possibility of error enter-
ng the sample must always be kept in mind. Throughout
nany years of pursuing this intricate business of audience

research technique, Nielsen has had to keep on its toes, constantly devising new procedures for lessening the margin o
error. The company's line of questioning is being mad
more sophisticated all the time. Since people are reluctan
to discuss income and education, often exaggerating both
ways have had to be found to eliminate hyperbole. For example, Nielsen will no longer ask an individual whether h
graduated from college. The current procedure is to ask th
number of years the respondent has attended.

Every figure appearing in the NTI or NSI is supported b
a sophisticated mathematical formula of reliability and va
lidity. The Nielsen people say they have found through th
years that there is more bias reported among the upper an
lower income groups than among the middle incomes. Th
extremes on either end of the income scale are the ones wh
most distort the amount they earn and the education the
have had. (Middle income is said to include those makin
between $5,000 and $10,000 a year.)

There are two other reasons besides the bias one, why rel
ability and validity factors must be worked into the fin
Nielsen results. One is that although meters accurately d
termine what channel is turned on, they do not let you kno
for sure whether the viewer is watching or doing somethin
else while the set is on. The second is that audience compo
tion is reported by the diary method, and research peop
find respondents are less accurate in the early morning ar
late at night when they fill in the diary forms.

What Is a Rating?

The rating figure is the percentage of the households,
children, or whatever group you want to measure that a

tuned to a particular TV program during an average quarter hour as compared to the *total* households, children, or whatever other group is being measured. In other words, the rating figure is the percentage faction viewing a specific program out of the total available television audience. If program X has received a rating of 2.5, it means that 2.5 per cent of the total available audience watched program X during an average quarter hour the program was on.

When we talk about the *entire range of television programs,* then the rating figures become known as *usage.* In Table 1, for instance, the portion of the chart titled *Television Usage* shows a figure of 48.9 under the column *Households* for the period Monday to Friday, 5:00 to 7:30 P.M. The interpretation of this usage figure is that for the period Monday through Friday, 5:00 to 7:30 P.M., 48.9 per cent of all of the television households in the country have their television sets turned on for the average quarter hour.

Every Nielsen report provides *quantitative* research estimates and is subject to misuse if somebody decides to assume that this quantitative research is actually *qualitative.* The error is made over and over again, sometimes intentionally. But the fact is that a Nielsen audience estimate of viewing tries to tell you what programs are being watched; it does not purport to tell what the viewers happen to think of the programs they are tuned to.

The Method of Survey

The Nielsen Company uses two methods to gather its figures. Each method acts as a check and balance against the others. The meter system is used to determine the levels of household viewing, or television usage. Meters are hooked

TABLE 1. TELEVISION VIEWING EACH WEEK IN THE PERIOD JANUARY 12–FEBRUARY 22, 1970*

A. Average number of hours viewed by children

Period of Usage	*Ages 2–5*	*Ages 6–11*
Monday-Friday, 5–7:30 PM	5.33	4.84
Saturday, 7 AM–1 PM	2.45	2.13
Monday-Sunday, 7:30–11 PM	6.98	9.63

B. Percentages of television usage

Period of Usage	*Households*	*Children*	
		Ages 2–5	*Ages 6–11*
Monday-Friday, 7–7:30 PM	51.6	42.6	38.7
Saturday, 7 AM–1 PM	21.5	40.9	35.5
Monday-Sunday, 7:30–11 PM	64.3	28.5	39.3
Program Type†			
General drama	18.6	3.8	6.1
Suspense and mystery drama	20.2	8.3	11.7
Situation comedy	18.9	13.9	19.1
Western	22.0	9.6	11.0
Variety	20.2	8.5	10.3
Quiz and audience participation	16.8	10.7	14.1
Feature films	19.4	5.2	9.6
Children's weekend	7.4	15.1	12.6

SOURCE: Nielsen National Audience Demographics Report.

* The Nielsen data cited are derived from Nielsen television audience measurements, and like the data in reports of these measurements, are estimate of the size and makeup of TV audiences and other characteristics of tele vision usage. The amounts and percentages as used here should not b regarded as a representation by Nielsen that the measurements are exac mathematical values.

† Prime time except for children's weekend entry.

onto selected television sets and each meter records ever time its user changes channels. The meter films periodicall are collected and analyzed by computer. The diary metho is used to determine audience composition. Selected households are invited to fill diaries on a daily basis. The diaries are periodically collected, tabulated, and fed into the computer for analysis.

On the basis of U.S. census figures Nielsen designs a master sample, the current version of which consists of 72,000 households. Through a complicated procedure designed to achieve a random sample, the firm picks what it calls sampling points. It knows, for example, precisely the house it wants to measure, the block it is in, even the address. Then it contacts the resident to see whether he will cooperate. Every year the research company must update the sample because houses are demolished, people move away, etcetera. Checks are made annually to see whether the same houses should be included in the forthcoming samplings. The selection of houses is on a random basis, and it is said each household in the country has a theoretical opportunity to participate in the poll.

The Nielson company first obtains from government records demographic information about families, including such facts as the number and ages of children in a given household, the occupation and probable income of the head of the household. Nielsen next interviews the family members person-to-person and may invite them to join the analyzing game. If this is agreeable, Nielsen sends them a diary every two weeks on which they will indicate quarter hour by quarter hour what TV program everybody is viewing.

Nielsen will force a change of household sampling of wenty to thirty per cent each year. Most families who sign p with the research company agree either to take part in the metering procedure or to keep the diary from three to five years. Beyond the normal annual twenty to thirty per cent turnover in sampling, some people move away, houses are demolished, and other changes occur, so that in actuality the changeover in the various samplings can far exceed the "forced" turnover.

Few Nielsen sample householders have been known to retire on the company's incentive plan. For the privilege of borrowing your nose to count, Nielsen will pay you a thrifty sum. If you allow the company to attach a meter to your TV set, every time you mail back the recording device and reinsert a fresh, unregistered one, two quarters fall into your hand from the recording cartridge. You are also entitled to fifty per cent repair bills if your set goes wacky. Diary keepers are similarly rewarded. It is well to remember that it is not the money that counts, but the way you play the game.

How Much Television Do Children Watch?

When adults learn the number of hours a week that children watch television, a good many of them are rather startled. Children aged two to five look at the TV tube on the average 28.4 hours every week; those between six and eleven average 23.6 hours a week (see Table 2). Averaging both age groups, we find that kids are watching television twelve hundred hours, or about the equivalent of one and two-thirds months a year. By any yardstick that is a good deal of visual exercise.

Every few years Nielsen prepares what it calls a quintile chart. This chart (See Table 2) divides children into two groups (ages 2–5 and ages 6–11) and each of these groups into fifths by the degree of their television viewing. The latest

TABLE 2. AVERAGE NUMBER OF HOURS PER WEEK VIEWED BY CHILDREN, NOVEMBER 1966 (IN QUINTILES)

Quintile	*Ages 2–5*	*Ages 6–11*
1 (heaviest)	49.2	41.9
2	30.8	26.7
3	20.9	19.2
4	12.8	12.7
5 (lightest)	2.4	3.8
Composite 1966	23.2	20.9
Composite November–December 1969	28.4	23.6
Composite January–February 1970	30.41	25.49

SOURCE: Nielsen Television Index, Report on Television Usage.

chart, compiled in 1966, shows that among the two to five age group, the heaviest viewing quintile averaged 49.2 hours a week, while the lightest viewing quintile averaged only 2.4 hours a week. Correspondingly, the heaviest watching among the six to eleven age group averaged 41.9 hours a week, with the lightest quintile averaging 3.8 hours. The Nielsen chart also gives composite viewing for both groups since 1966. One prime factor accounting for the differentiation among the quintiles appears to be parental supervision or lack of it.

The heaviest watching periods for young people can be seen on the chart (Table 1) indicating average hours viewed per week. Here we find that Monday through Friday, 5:00 to 7:30 P.M., the two to fives are viewing 5.33 hours on the average each week; the older group watches only a fraction less during this same time period. On Saturdays, during the six-hour cartoon block, the two to fives are gulping television down, viewing 2.45 hours on the average; the older children average only slightly less. During the week, beginning Monday and running straight through to the following Sunday, children between two and five see 6.98 hours of TV on the average during the time period 7:30 to 11:00 P.M. In the same period of prime time, six- to eleven-year-olds watch almost three hours more than their younger brothers and sisters.

In Table 1 under *Television Usage,* it is possible to determine the number of children who are watching TV by age group for the same heavy viewing periods already discussed. The key factors missing are these: the total number of two- to five-year-olds in TV homes in the United States at the time these data were analyzed (estimated at 15,650,000), and the total number of six to elevens (24,910,000). To calculate household usage, it should be borne in mind that the total number of TV homes in the nation at that time was estimated at 58,500,000. So, as they are prone to say in math books, it is obvious that multiplying the population of the age group in question by the usage in the table will supply you with the total number of children tuned in at the time period you are wondering about.

Viewing by the Disadvantaged Child

The belief is widely held that children in the lower income families are among the heaviest watchers of TV. And the decriers of violence never let us forget how aggressive behavioral patterns are being learned by these unsupervised kids. In any viewing period you may select, you find that *children in the low income households comprise the lowest shares of composite viewing* (the total of men, women, teens and children in all income brackets). For example, in every the heavy prime time periods (Monday through Saturday, 7:30 to 11:00 P.M.) the children in the low income group comprise only eleven per cent of the total audience. TV set ownership is lowest, too, among low income households. Interestingly enough, the general viewing habits of the upper and lower classes is about the same in hours but different from the standpoint of program choice.

Nielsen lists programs by popularity in its national rankings (Table 3). In analyzing the table, it is important to make the distinction between the column marked *by estimated household audiences* and that marked *by estimated child audiences*. Both columns show the popularity rankings for the period October 13, 1969, to November 23, 1969. Rankings in each instance show the top twenty television programs on the air during the two-week period under investigation. The *Household* column refers only to the measurement of sets across the country that were turned on to each specific program; it completely disregards audience composition. The program ranking by children, however, shows a completely different pattern. We see here in this comparison that the overall rating figure is not the holy number many people think it is; it is essential to study the demographic charts as well to make an intelligent statement about the viewing habits of children or any other group. It is not enough to hold up Nielsen rankings by household before an audience and say, "Look at that, folks, *Gunsmoke* — that violent show — is ranked number nine in popularity." Somebody is apt to come up behind you who knows how to read these charts and point out that on the chart of children's rankings *Gunsmoke* did not even make the top twenty programs in popularity.

TABLE 3. GENERAL PROGRAM RANKINGS

A. National, by estimated child audiences (aged 2–11)*
January 12–February 22, 1970

Rank	*Program*	*Average Audience (in thousands)*
1	He's Your Dog, Charlie Brown (special)	17,370
2	Born Free (special)	15,080
3	Harlem Globetrotters (special)	12,930
4	Ringling Brothers Circus (special)	11,270
5	Bewitched (evening)	11,170
6	Uncle Sam Magoo (special)	11,030
7	My Three Sons	10,120
8	Courtship of Eddie's Father	9,640
9	Bob Hope Christmas Show (special)	9,490
10	Nanny & the Professor	9,390
11	Wonderful World of Disney	9,350
12	The Monkees	9,220
13	That Girl (evening)	9,110
14	Archie Comedy Hour	8,860
15	The Brady Bunch	8,840
16	H. R. Pufnstuf	8,740
17	Bill Cosby	8,690
18	Scooby-Doo, Where Are You?	8,640
19	Pink Panther	8,480
20	Family Affair	8,460

SOURCE: Nielsen Television Index.
* Projected by computer.

Referring back to usage by program type (Table 1), by far the most popular program type for all children is the situation comedy. Two to fives prefer next, in descending order, westerns, variety shows, quiz programs, mystery dramas, feature films, and general dramas. The six- to eleven-year-olds, after situation comedy, show preference for westerns, variety shows, mystery dramas, quiz programs, fea-

TABLE 3. GENERAL PROGRAM RANKINGS (CONTINUED)
B. National, by estimated household audiences
January 12–February 22, 1970

Rank	*Program*
1	Bob Hope Christmas Show (special)
2	Bob Hope (special)
3	Born Free (special)
4	Ringling Brothers Circus (special)
5	He's Your Dog, Charlie Brown (special)
6	Rowan & Martin Special (special)
7	Danny Thomas Special (special)
8	Harlem Globetrotters (special)
9	Gunsmoke
9	Rowan & Martin Laugh-In
11	Many Moods of Perry Como (special)
12	Here's Lucy
13	World of the Beaver
14	Family Affair
14	Mayberry-R.F.D.
16	Bonanza
16	Red Skelton
18	Marcus Welby, M.D.
19	National Geographic Special (special)
20	Hawaii Five-O

SOURCE: Nielsen Television Index.

ture films, and general dramas. The claim that children are systematically drawn to mystery fails to be supported by the facts.

Let us assume for a moment that the critics of television have merit in their case that TV is planting the seeds of aggression in young viewers. Those who have appeared before Congressional investigations to inveigh against the medium have hurled their invectives at the *networks only,* not

TABLE 3. GENERAL PROGRAM RANKINGS (CONTINUED)
C. In New York City, by estimated child audiences (aged 2–11) January 15–February 11, 1970*

Rank	*Program*	*Station*	*Average Audience (in thousands)*
1	World of Disney	Network	1,005
2	The Munsters (Monday-Friday)	Independent	992
3	I Love Lucy (Saturday)	Independent	989
4	H. R. Pufnstuf	Network	929
5	The Monkees	Network	902
6	The Flintstones (Sunday)	Independent	880
7	Ringling Brothers Circus (special)	Network	843
8	I Love Lucy (Monday-Friday)	Independent	832
9	The Brady Bunch	Network	794
10	My Three Sons	Network	788
11	Lassie	Network	787
12	Pink Panther	Network	780
13	Jonny Quest	Network	772
14	Superman (Saturday)	Network	755
15	Batman (Monday-Friday)	Independent	751
16	Lost in Space (Monday-Friday)	Independent	738
17	Here Comes the Grump	Network	717
18	Wonderama	Independent	715
19	Archie Comedy Hour	Network	710
20	Courtship of Eddie's Father	Network	703

SOURCE: Nielsen Television Index.

* A number of specials appearing on the Nielsen total U.S. ranking list were aired after the measurement period in New York and therefore are not included even though their audience sizes may have qualified them to be.

against the local stations. Again, let us assume the networks were suddenly to "purify" themselves, removing all traces of what critics call objectionable programming. Television would still not be "cleansed" because the syndication process would perpetuate the older objectionable programs over the local stations. Generally speaking, it is the local stations that have been least willing to police their own programming, citing economics as a prime reason. They have air time to fill and with low budgets they pick up the old network shows which can be had at low prices. We stress this point because in the metropolitan market of New York six of the top twenty programs were carried not by the networks but by independent stations (see Table 3). Yet it should also be clear that among those six local, independent stations the programs ranked most popular were not programs filled with violence.

The Politics of Ratings

High ratings ensure a large share of advertising revenue for a network or individual TV station. The advertiser is made to feel he is getting the best buy for his money, that for each advertising dollar he is reaching more potential consumers. It is not an uncommon business practice for some stations to switch rating services if one particular service (using different samples and procedures) can provide higher numbers than another research company.

Some children's performers complain bitterly that new shows are scrapped frequently because many TV executives and advertisers do not understand the rating concepts at all and consider the figures absolutes. New shows have to be given time to build audiences; success does not generally come overnight. Some research firms supply what are called overnight figures, and when they are applied to a new program, the show may appear to be doing poorly. On the basis of a few "opening night" ratings, a good television program may go the way of the scrap heap. Ratings can also offer a convenient way to drop a popular program, if for one reason or another the program performers have fallen out with management yet are under contract. The program can be moved into a known poor viewing time against strong opposition in such a way as to induce a flop. Then it's "Sorry, Charlie, here only the successful shows can stay!"

8 THE TV SET: WHAT ARE THEY LEARNING?

Shortly after the mission of Apollo 12, one of my young son's playmates dropped by the house to show us with pride a crayon drawing he had made. It was a drawing of the lunar module lifting off from the surface of the moon, orange flame spewing from each of the small rocket engines. The six-year-old artist had depicted even the rocket stages, as well as craters on the moon and the contrast between the blackness of space and the sun-drenched lunar surface. What amazed us was the accuracy of detail in the drawing, an accuracy made possible by television's thorough space coverage.

Today's young television generation will talk to you about things the pretelevision generation never conceived of. They will tell you about the latest frontal systems in the weather picture and they will ask you questions about the confusing turns of politics. Their world is as broad as the infinite horizon of the television camera. It would be hard to deny that much of what children see and know they are acquiring from the TV set. But there are some stalwart souls around who insist this is nonsense, that children are learning little or nothing of value from television.

One of these holdouts is Donald Barr, headmaster of the Dalton Schools in New York. True to the educationist's stovepipe philosophy, he is suspicious of electrons which behave in erratic ways and are seemingly antiintellectual in themselves. "Youngsters are bombarded from earliest infancy onward with high-potency stimuli of low intellectual organization. . . . This makes it very difficult to get things with high intellectual organization with low-pressure stimuli." The rough translation of that educationism is that TV entertainment is providing so much competition for kids' attention their reading has fallen off. Would an educationist concede for one moment that children are learning from television, that the medium can be a source of knowledge? "No, I would not," replies the Dalton official. "Television gives you vicarious experience, but it does not give you any critical or conceptual framework by which to understand this experience . . . it is inherently a short-circuiting of imaginative and rational processes."

Harvard's Bigelow professor of education and developmental psychology, Gerald Lesser, will not look at television through the monocle of intellectual snobbery. "What the medium can do," Lesser says with great enthusiasm, "is to show the kids something of the world they're not likely to see, something they may perhaps never have an opportunity to see."

Any truly scientific exploration to study the extent of television learning would require locating communities in the United States where TV does not exist at all. That would provide what researchers consider necessary control conditions to make possible a comparison between learning in communities with TV and in those where the medium has no exposure. But television so blankets the country it is virtually impossible to find TV-proof regions anywhere. There are, however, some isolated pockets here and there where clusters of households exist that are without even a single television set. In some towns in Mississippi, quite a few homes without TV lie in the shadows of homes with one or more sets. Teachers there report that the children who live in the TV households are much more alert and "with the world" than are the children residing in homes without television.

Most of the information children pick up from the tube amounts to incidental learning. It is the kind of knowledge they may acquire simply by watching programs they find entertaining. This is not meant to imply that shows that are built on pure fluff and visual gimmickry automatically will offer the child an intellectual challenge. The point is that it is not necessary to hit a child over the head and say, "Now learn this!" The process of learning can be a lot more subtle, and the medium offers an excellent opportunity to stretch young minds.

A Question of Passivity

Parents responding to our survey often said they were afraid the many hours spent in front of the television set were somehow making their kids passive. The correlative fear is that TV is helping to build a generation of spectators. "Passivity," though, is a vague term, and we should examine its various shadings.

We may first of all think of passivity with respect to the thinking process. There is the child in front of the set—apparently motionless and half asleep. It is logical to suspect the child's mind has come to a full stop. On this score, psychologist Edward Palmer of the Children's Television Workshop comments, "You know, we've come to think of *active* participation as a kind of motor thing — the idea that you have to keep running all around. But I don't believe that in dealing with normal human beings we have to watch them push a button to know something is happening inside." Dr. Palmer shrugs off that school of psychology that insists that only overt behavioral signs tell whether something active and worthwhile is going on. That is what he chooses to call "psychology based on pigeon or rat behavior." Dr. Palmer says he has seen enough evidence to know that kids' minds can be really turned on by TV, despite the fact that they may sit motionless or appear bound in lethargy. He explains that there are different styles of behavior. The little ones who jump up and talk to the set and the ones who sit back and look to all the world as though nothing is going on inside. A child may be viewing alone, and when he thinks no one is watching he may get up and do all sorts of things. He may perform an imitation of a teen-age dance in front of the set or talk back to the performer. But if he gets the impression he is being watched, he is more likely to sit down quietly and become a little embarrassed. Little children learn very early to suppress these free kinds of responses.

We may come to think of passivity in a creative sense or from a standpoint of initiative. Television, according to many teachers, does curb the creative spirit. Everything is presented to children in very concrete fashion with little left to the imagination. The result is that more and more small children are asking for specific, concrete instructions in their artwork. And the general feeling among many teachers is that a lot of the imaginative energies of young children are being contained; perhaps the creative process in some way is being sapped by overexposure to television. Individual initiative can be diluted because the medium is often relied on to spark direction and purpose. And perhaps in this sense headmaster Barr's concern with the erosion of the imaginative process does have merit.

People have also come to speak of passivity in the sense that it may lead to a jaded palate. This fear is unfounded. If anything, quite the opposite appears to take place. It has been found that bright children, especially, become interested in a wider range of subjects as a result of viewing than children who have not been exposed to TV in remote areas around the country.

What about the perplexing question about today's young people turning into a generation of spectators? Psychiatrist Paul Syracuse rejects the whole idea. "I think there are many more activists *now* . . . and I feel positively strong about that. The young people who have been raised on television are becoming more actively involved in political issues. Because I think they understand more — they have more information fed to them." Dr. Syracuse continues, "I also think they know more about politics at fifteen than we ever did. I know of a kid who at fourteen wants to run for mayor. Of course, that's absurd. But to hear him talk, why he knows more about political issues at his age than supposedly well-seasoned politicians!"

Preschoolers who watch television extensively show a decided advantage in vocabulary buildup over light television viewers by the time they enroll in school. But unless the impetus stimulated by TV is supported and reinforced by parental assistance later on, the early advantage in word power seems to decline.

The question of whether television stimulates or blunts enthusiasm for reading puzzles many parents—and not without good reason. The issue has been hotly debated from both sides of the aisle by television's supporters and its detractors. Librarians have told us that the demand for books by children is definitely on the rise and they believe this increasing thirst for books is due at least in part to television. TV, according to the librarians, piques a child's curiosity to look things up in books for more detail.

Educated parents often feel that knowledge that is transmitted by television is somehow more primitive than that which is transmitted in print. They therefore do not want their children to bypass the broader culture of the book for TV, and so they complain that the television medium is taking their kids away from reading. But most children cannot be taken away from a literary culture that was not part of their lives to begin with. In Western Europe, as well as in America, the people who most enthusiastically accepted television were the very ones who never embraced the culture of the book. The more highly educated, here and abroad, were the people who offered the greatest resistance to television. That is why psychiatrist Bruno Bettelheim of the University of Chicago makes the following point. He says that while television has widened the horizons of nonbook readers, the highly literate among us illogically fear TV will narrow the nonreader's cultural tradition. For instance, Donald Barr emphatically denies that TV stimulates reading. Says Barr, "What it does is stimulate casting your eye over the page, and that is a far different thing from reading. Children may pick up and leaf through more books, but what they do looks to me less and less like reading every year."

Dr. Bettelheim tells us that psychologically there are great differences between culture acquired through the book and through TV. This is due to the more immediate impact of television with its simplified, dramatic form as compared to what we read in the book in more complex form, with much subtler shadings. "TV captures the imagination but does not liberate it," Dr. Bettelheim says. "A good book at once stimulates and frees the mind." He reminds the educationists that probably never again will the printed word be our prime source of information. The printed word, he says, will have to share this function with television and the other mass media. He views the book and the television medium as equally worthy competitors for man's mind (from Bruno Bettelheim, "Parents vs. Television," *Redbook,* 122, no. 1, November 1963).

Television can serve as a reading substitute for the young child who is not so much concerned about detail as he is interested in broad, general concepts of knowledge. As the child grows older his sources of knowledge expand to include the peer group, schoolwork, church activities and the like. At this point there is more demand on the child's part for *detail,* the kind of information television cannot present because of its rapid transmission and time problems. Moreover, there is also more need for closer examination of the facts, a slower process that entails review and reconsideration. This kind of information, he learns, can be gotten not from television but from printed material, and so he begins to rely more and more heavily on books as he grows older.

Young children who are going through the process of learning to read are likely to remain with television as a prime source of knowledge and entertainment. As reading proficiency improves, children turn more to the printed word for an expansion of knowledge. And when they see books being read on television as well as by adults at home, that further stimulates interest in reading. Most experts agree that children raised in an environment where the family shows strong reading habits can generally be expected to become good readers sooner or later, regardless of early television viewing habits.

Generally speaking, television appears to exert neither a positive nor a negative effect on the school grades of younger children; the effect is simply a neutral one. Parents of older children occasionally mentioned in our survey that, if anything, TV appeared to exert a deleterious effect on their children's grades. They attributed the cause to watching programs instead of spending time on homework. That is a disciplinary problem which will be discussed in chapter 18.

How TV Is Changing Teaching Methods

The eyes have had it! A sure sign, say school teachers, that it is Monday morning. The eyes of the pupils (or perhaps the other way around) keep staring straight ahead, almost as though they do not see anything. TV weekend syndrome, or Monday morning hangover, is what is happening. The bloodshot, dazed look on the faces of some of the children are telltale indications the kids have been staring at television for two solid days. Teachers interviewed in West Orange, New Jersey, see the problem as one of parental overpermissiveness, of allowing children to stay up too long and watch television without adequate supervision. There is a widespread feeling that television may be developing selective listening patterns in a number of children. Since they are able to change TV channels so readily when their interest drops, they appear to be adapting this listening technique to the classroom as well. If the child loses interest in the subject at hand, he simply turns his teacher off. The West Orange educators, noting the dilemma, are developing new teaching methods to cope with it.

Speech teachers are now given special assignments to visit the schools to teach children the lost art of active listening, to stretch what some have called their *boredom spans.* Then the classroom teacher steps in with her own follow-up program. Teachers are beginning to feel the strong silent competition from the medium. The traditional teaching methods are no longer effective to get student response. In a sense, elements of show business have entered the classroom. Teachers are discovering it is no longer sufficient to stand in front of the room and talk. They now have to move around a lot, bring in visual aids that the children can handle, taste and smell. The best of them plan their lessons around television programs that spark the kids' attention, find TV ideas they can adapt to their own classrooms and work at new ways of switching the "turned off" children back on again. If television executives must learn to incorporate educational elements in their programs, turnabout in the classroom seems only fair play.

9 LET'S TALK ABOUT VIOLENCE

The American conscience is bleeding from the aorta and we are waving our hands about wildly searching for the correct pressure points. Political assassinations and senseless tribal-like murders have evoked a hysteria that seeks an immediate answer to the questions of how do we end violence and where does it begin.

Not so many years ago, when people noted the crime curve turning upward, smoking was blamed for criminal behavior, the corruption of youth, and other social ills. Of course such views may seem ridiculous now, but we must remember that they were held by many sensible citizens. And again, when movies came along the boney fingers of accusation were pointed at them. The anxieties voiced were not only those of cranks, but of clergymen, judges, teachers, and other educated people. So it should not be all that astounding that television has been brought before the grand jury of public opinion, with many respected people convinced of its guilt.

One of my colleagues at CBS News — a well-known, respected correspondent who would blush at the mention of his name — is convinced that television to a large extent *is* responsible for making children violent. He told us, "I don't care what facts you come up with or what conclusions you reach, I'll continue to believe as I do, because that is my opinion." An otherwise bright man, he shows he is just as likely to fall into a human trap as the rest of us, ready and willing to rationalize his feelings and predispositions, even in the light of fresh contradictory evidence.

The search for a thread linking violence in the streets to violence on television has over the last two decades led to four major Congressional investigations. This has been in keeping with the American political tradition of calling for a governmental "study" or investigation when a seemingly unfathomable problem confronts us and we need a ready, instant solution that will take the heat off the politicians. Studies such as these rarely solve the problems; they act as safety valves, convincing the public that situations are under control. Ironically, such studies often proliferate an abundance of misinformation under the seal of governmental good housekeeping.

In an appearance before the Eisenhower violence commission, the director of CBS research, Dr. Joseph Klapper, commented, "These studies are apparently much more widely discussed than they are read . . . It is a great misfortune." There is also a fascinating contradiction between what people who are suspicious of TV's role in aggression *say* about television and what they *do* about it. More and more parents talk about the harmful effect TV violence may be having on their children, yet how many of these parents control the use of their TV sets?

Psychological experts tell us that violence essentially is part of our marrow, something we must somehow learn how to live with and control. One of the mistakes we often make trying to comprehend the phenomenon of violence is to assume that the rules of *logic* apply. They do not. We are not dealing here with a sequence of ideas but with a *nervous system*. Experimental psychologists are busy devising laboratory experiments to explain patterns of aggression, but there are assumptions they make which do not hold up.

One problem, explains the noted Philadelphia clinical psychologist and author Barry Bricklin, is that research makes it impossible to draw conclusions, "because experiments are designed in a way that you can't design real life situations. You simply can't re-create in the lab what you see in practice." Experimenters also have a propensity to draw "logical" conclusions.

Whenever we hear of another bizarre murder we wring our hands and mutter about this age of increased violence. It certainly *seems* to be true, but then we have to stop and consider the proposition, weighing it carefully. On the plus side, we have given up burning witches and we do not even hold public hangings, as they do in Baghdad. But on the minus side, the fact is we have always been violent. We settled our disputes on the frontier with guns. We have had an inglorious history with our black brothers since the early days of slavery. The difference is we didn't used to talk very much about those matters. Social pressures to do so were absent, and there were not a lot of reporters poking around in search of good, juicy stories. The rapid dissemination of news has brought to our attention many things that in years past would have gone unnoticed and forgotten. Population has grown to the point where we are now told by governmental health officials that the increase of newborns is adding to our gigantic pollution problems. The suffocating conditions of impacted living set the stage for increased violence; we are literally at one another's throats. Moreover, the jump in sheer numbers of people statistically increases the pool of psychotics prone to overt violent behavior.

Our psychological consultants point out that our natural violent tendencies must be given a chance to discharge at minimal levels. But what we have done is continually cut out the harmless discharge routes, as though it is somehow connected to the problem of runaway inflation in the country. Long before our children even reach the age of reason, there we are telling them to play "nicely." And we set up a list of "don'ts" with which we are all quite familiar: don't hit, don't swear, don't scream back at the other kids. Hardly anybody lives in the country anymore, so most children do not have an opportunity to chop wood, lead the plow horse about, or even carve initials in a tree.

Recently, our young son came home very angry at a playmate who would not let him look into a new telescope. He walked over to a drawing board and scribbled all over it, labeled it "an angry picture," and hung it up on the refrigerator. We might have torn the picture down and frustrated him, saying something like "Refrigerators are not for hanging." But that was a harmless discharge tactic he had used to rid himself of pent-up hostility.

The generation of children who by twelve or thirteen were compelled to be self-supporting had no time for rebellion. Besides, the prevailing attitudes were too rigid to allow for social change. Now affluence has done away with child labor, and the young people are sufficiently uptight to demand changes in our social patterns as well as in our institutions. If they feel defeated, they may opt out of society as hippies. But they may press on, frequently exploding into violence. For them, violence seems to be a shortcut to gaining some objective. But the revolt shows they have not learned how to deal with their own violence. As psychiatrist Bruno Bettelheim suggests, violence is so primitive in nature it is completely unsuitable for getting us the subtler satisfactions we want. That, concludes Bettelheim, marks the beginning of man's becoming a socialized human being. Again, it all traces back to our initial dealings with our youngsters. We have no business simply teaching young children idyllic stories that are devoid of life's essential emotions. We should not be afraid to tell them that people are sometimes angry at one another, that they sometimes quarrel, but that they can still learn to live together successfully by coping with their own violent feelings and similar feelings in others.

In suppressing our children's violent tendencies, we are simply allowing the aggression to build up into huge thunderclouds which can be expected one day to shower us with frenzy and unexpected lightning. These outbursts can be quite spectacular and by their very appearance lead us to believe ours is indeed a more violent age. Our immediate reaction is perhaps to clamor for a curbing of smaller and smaller eruptions of violence. We take away play guns many psychiatrists regard as safety valves or discharge routes, thereby continuing to suppress the natural violent nature of our kids. And we have been getting extremely efficient at building thunderclouds. So what it comes down to is that in an increasingly impacted age, with more and more people living on top of one another, we keep cutting off safe discharge routes for aggression, unknowingly building up the forces of violence to the boiling point. Then many of us turn around in a state of confusion and wonderment, asking if perhaps that inanimate but occasionally blaring TV set in the corner is not really the culprit who has done us all in.

Americans have a special fondness for crash programs of all sorts. We like our answers to complicated problems to come quickly, economically, and, if possible, in convenient, pleasant-tasting tablet form. Once we are motivated to do something we move with alacrity, as the space program has dramatized. Until recently, we were not strongly motivated to trace possible connections between TV violence and violence in our lives. But now that we are, we would like rapid, conclusive answers to our questions concerning this issue. Unhappily, we are thoroughly frustrated in the matter because we are seeking solutions not to technological problems but to human ones. These problems are not readily solved in crash programs, however expensive; rapidity does not make for validity, and the variables in dealing with the human organism are too complex to conform to swift generalization. Yet that does not stop many experimental psychologists from trying.

In 1958, a British group, the Nuffield Foundation, completed a four-year-long study to determine television's impact on children. The published report, *Television and the Child,* by psychologists H. T. Himmelweit, A. N. Oppenheim and Pamela Vince (Oxford: Oxford University Press, 1958) touched on, but did not concentrate on, the subject of TV violence. Despite the length of the study, the authors admitted their evidence in this area was incomplete and inconclusive. In their conclusions, the British psychologists reported that "the constant display of aggression by both the criminal and the upholder of the law would make an impact on children sensitized to such clues." Certain children are likely to be triggered by something they see on TV and to behave in some violent manner. Psychiatrist Irving Markowitz, reflecting the majority viewpoint among our experts, counters that implication. In order for this to happen even with a psychotic, he says, "you would have to hit a particular point of sensitivity and then emphasize the very point that someone wants to conceal. I don't think television does that." Dr. Paul Syracuse adds that if you are concerned about triggering psychotics, anything can do it; why blame TV? More likely to trigger certain children to overt violent acts are incidents closely related to their life situations, an argument between the child's mother and father or perhaps something a brother or sister says to the child. Reporting on the effect of TV westerns and crime programs, the Nuffield psychologists conclude, "We did not find the viewers were any more aggressive or maladjusted than the control groups."

It should be noted that in light of the absence of extensive studies on children's TV, the British investigation has had to serve as a basis for much of the current literature in this field. Writers using the report as a basis have tended to generalize about "children" perhaps without realizing that the Nuffield study utilized in the main, older children, ten to fourteen. The sampling of very young children was minute and not considered by the Nuffield group to be sufficiently representative. Therefore, much of the literature on children's TV still reflects inaccuracy of impact studies on younger children. We should also recall that very young children do not prefer watching westerns or mystery thrillers, as so many of us have assumed. Both younger and older children overwhelmingly choose situation comedies and variety shows over the kinds of programs we have been so alarmed about.

In 1969, the National Broadcasting Company quietly launched what may well turn out to be the most comprehensive study of television violence yet undertaken. This investigation, costing a half million dollars, was to stretch over a period of five years. According to NBC research vice president Dr. Thomas Coffin, the purpose is "to determine the social influences of television on children, and, in particular, the relationship of television's influence on them." The main thrust of the work will be to examine the effect of television violence on children's behavior. What this means, then, is that while the concentrated effort by NBC would be on TV aggression, the other possible influences of the medium would also be looked at. During the first year the research team fixed its attention on developing methods and tools for investigation. The field work, begun in the spring of 1970, was to continue for a total of three years. The fifth year will be spent analyzing results of the vast field studies. Subjects will range in age between five and seventeen, and comparative studies will be made on ghetto and middle-class children. The chief researcher, sociologist Ronald Milavsky, tells us that the field work is being conducted in two undisclosed cities, neither of them in the East. Dr. Milavsky contends the higher crime rate cities are not in the East. He says the NBC work is to be carried out in *consultation* with psychologists, criminologists, and others.

Perhaps one of the weakest links in most of these studies is that the research is usually done on a consulting basis between members of the different related academic disciplines. We believe the effort should be more than a consulative study; it should be carried out by a board of experts, each having an equally shared responsibility in the final product. And certainly such boards should provide room for representatives of the psychiatric community.

The NBC people have encountered the same situation we did when we began carrying out our own investigation in preparation of this book. The NBC researchers feel that the quietness of approach in the investigation will help ensure more reliable results. The hope is that if subjects do not realize the actual purpose for which they are being tested, they are less likely to give inhibited responses to questions. Avoiding the glare of publicity, too, perhaps can help researchers overcome the poor cooperation they have been getting so often from school administrators and parents.

The national hysteria over violence in America has convinced a good many of us that television is, in fact, the chief villain. Those who accept TV's guilt search continually for the evidence in every program they see. Ten years ago, the president of the National Association for Better Broadcasting, Mrs. Clara Logan, sat in on the Dodd hearings on juvenile delinquency, reciting her count to the lawmakers: "For a single week in November 1960 we witnessed the following: 144 murders, 143 attempted murders, 52 justified killings, 14 cases of drugging, 12 jail breaks, 36 robberies, 6 thefts, 13 kidnappings, 6 burglaries, 7 cases of torture, 6 extortion cases, 5 blackmails, 11 planned murders, 4 attempted lynchings, and 1 massacre scene with hundreds killed." The writers and television producers who sat through the body count could not convince Mrs. Logan that she was "reaching" for evidence to convict TV and that she had overlooked the essential point. Children, they insisted, can comprehend the *whole story,* that they are not sitting there registering every violent scene on magnetic tape ready for instant replay.

In all this time, we have done little to check the real root cause of crime and violence in the country, so it is not surprising that the number of TV violent scene counters spread like a rash. For a lot of people, dissecting TV stories into violent parts has become an interesting game; unfortunately, it proves no more today than it ever did. We do not mean to imply that the kinds of programs referred to above are necessarily those we consider worthy of continuance. Our contention is simply that the violent sequences on television are not sure-fire triggering devices for imitative behavioral response.

The television crime counters are all the more confident of their case against TV when they hear about the experimentations of psychologist Dr. Albert Bandura of Stanford University. Dr. Bandura has been a star witness before Senate crime investigators, and his research has been widely quoted, though not thoroughly understood. One of these — the famous Bobo doll experiment — appears in most of the literature on children's TV and illustrates how the results are often misconstrued.

The experimenter picked three matched groups of preschoolers for the Bobo doll exercise. The first group observed a real-life adult striking a large rubber Bobo doll with a mallet for ten minutes. His second group observed the same action, but this time it had been filmed. The third group of youngsters served as a control and saw neither the real-life action nor the filmed version. Next, all three groups were led into a playroom where there were some harmless toys as well as a mallet and a replica of the Bobo doll. Dr. Bandura reported that those who had seen either the real-life or filmed version of the Bobo doll being struck imitated the action of the woman, who incidentally accompanied her "aggressive behavior" by shouting such things as "Pow!" and "Sockeroo!" They were so imitative, said Dr. Bandura, that they also shouted such things as "Pow!" and "Sockeroo!" The conclusion Dr. Bandura left to the Senate investigators; they concluded that children can *learn* violence from television. The inference many drew from this and a host of other experiments that Dr. Bandura related was that children who see violence on television surely will repeat that behavior under the appropriate circumstances. It took Dr. Bandura a long time to clarify his statement that he did not mean to imply that *learning* aggression means reverting to *aggressive behavior*. But the crime counters had heard enough. They rushed from the hearing rooms convinced the evidence was now all in.

Our psychiatric experts say that it is important to realize that while the children may learn this TV aggression, it may first channel into their thought processes and then into their play. But beyond that, the consensus is that it *does not translate from play into behavior*. Boston psychiatrist John Spillane: "I think this kind of observation could lead to hostile behavior imitation *in play*. When the kids play cowboys and Indians, for instance, they may perhaps have tomahawks, might conceivably hit each other lightly. If they're five or more, they know not to hit hard. It's a tap. I just do not believe the ordinary child would infiltrate this kind of behavior from a play situation to actual performance."

We asked Dr. Bandura if he himself expects such a translation from play to performance. His response was that he is only talking about *learning* aggression, not behavior responses. Dr. Bandura went on to add that if he had really meant to prove behavioral aspects, he would have to sit down and design a whole completely new set of experiments. The Bobo doll experiment, he remarked, proved only that aggression can be learned. But a lot of people have taken Dr. Bandura to mean that watching TV violence leads to violent behavior, and that is *not* what he is saying at all.

Others have lent support to Dr. Bandura's work. That is to say, they have set about proving that aggression can be learned, and again people accept their experiments as added proof that TV violence leads directly to violence in the streets. Critics of the Bandura experiments point out that the learning situation is itself quite artificial. It took place, in the case of the Bobo doll, immediately after a ten-minute exposure to a woman pummeling the toy. That kind of action can hardly be expected to be representative of a television sequence, and the children were immediately placed in a situation where the tools of the aggressive play (the mallet and doll) were furnished. Hardly a real-life situation.

Experimental psychologists taking part in these "aggression" experiments also have strange and unusual conceptions of aggression. Take the impressive-sounding experiment by Paul Mussen and Eldred Rutherford of the University of California, Berkeley ("Effects of Aggressive Cartoons on Children's Aggressive Play," *Journal of Abnormal and Social Psychology,* 1961)—guaranteed to send the shudders through any crime counter.

"The purpose of this study was to test the hypothesis that

exposure to aggressive fantasy in an animated cartoon may intensify children's impulses to aggression. Subjects were thirty-six first grade children, eighteen girls and eighteen boys, of middle class origin. The intensity of the child's aggressive impulses was inferred from his response to questions concerning desire to 'play with' a large yellow balloon held by a tester. The experimental findings clearly supported the major prediction that exposure to aggressive fantasy in an animated cartoon would stimulate children's behavior in play."

Death Comes to the Living Room

The specter of death is no stranger to the American living room: the killing of President John F. Kennedy, November 22, 1963; the murder of Lee Harvey Oswald, November 24, 1963; the assassination of Martin Luther King, April 4, 1968; the slaying of Senator Robert F. Kennedy, June 5, 1968; the funeral of President Dwight D. Eisenhower, March 28, 1969. It would seem entirely reasonable that the televised aftermath of death, and especially of assassination, must have left some psychic imprint on young impressionable minds.

Slightly more than half of the parents we interviewed reported that their children had reacted to the assassinations. A number said the youngsters had expressed sorrow for the children of the deceased. Many young television viewers were perplexed by the violence, questioning why a man had been shot. Five-year-old John later lost his grandfather and wanted to know when the grandfather's funeral would be televised. Six-year-old Martha was frightened every time she saw Sirhan Sirhan on the TV screen. An eight-year-old child reading a history book asked his mother who shot Roosevelt. And a nine-year-old girl supposed that if you were elected President, you would undoubtedly be killed. Three five-year-olds in Boston developed their own new game called "Shoot the President." The little boy who conceived of the game said to his playmate, Julie, "All right, you be the President." Julie wanted to know which one, Kennedy or Johnson. "Oh, Kennedy, you jerk," the boy replied, "he's the one who got shot." Julie began to cry; then the second little girl comforted her, saying, "Don't cry, Julie. I'll kill you and you kill me." The mother who reported this incident said the children had translated the assassination of John Kennedy into something they could understand. She said she had been depressed by the whole thing because as she watched the three children play she noted the reenactment was correct in every detail.

Two factors determined the extent of reaction in the youngsters. For one thing, television's visual imagery had left deep scars. For another, parental reaction to the assassinations may have acted as a reinforcement.

One mother told how, immediately after Dr. King was killed, she had strolled through the Boston Common to attend a rally with her husband and children. People were sitting about quietly, she said. "We told them [the children] that Martin Luther King had been shot, how everybody was sad, that he was a good man and didn't like fighting and violence. We told them how wicked it was that someone had shot him like this. The children listened and we went home. Four weeks later we went back to the Common to go on the swan boats, and our son David, who was just two, remembered the whole story. A lot of his reaction was probably because we had had the television set on and had *followed it with interest.*"

Some parents we spoke with said their children "were too young to react to the assassinations." Interestingly, the youngsters were in the same age range as those who reportedly displayed a reaction, which leads us to wonder if parents who reported "no reaction" were (1) insensitive to the children's reaction, or (2) projecting their own reactions on to their children.

Dr. Paul Syracuse believes the real hang-up with violence in the country was touched off by the shooting of the accused assassin Lee Harvey Oswald by Jack Ruby. "I think the effects of the assassination," says Dr. Syracuse, "are long-lasting on young children. They saw those horrible things on television and watched their parents react strongly in many cases. They could see the funerals and the mourning and what it did to people. It may help them in one respect . . . with understanding the concept of death . . . knowing that big, important people have been hurt and killed. I don't think the effects on the children are bad . . . but they are lasting."

Psychiatrist John Spillane says one of the factors that makes such an impression on the young is the contemporary aspect of the assassinations. "The children know that they have taken place today, somewhere . . . they may also realize that the slain man has a family . . . John Kennedy, Robert Kennedy, Martin Luther King . . . they all had kids. The funerals took place in familiar cities. They know the places . . . they have seen the White House, perhaps." It is the proximity in time and place that television underscores that leaves the imprint.

Dr. Irving Markowitz shows us another dimension to the television funerals and assassinations. He says television has exposed the tawdry side of life to young people, "I think some of the falsities that were generated around the deaths, some of the reverential concerns. I think the kids picked up some of the hypocrisy of the mourners. They see a guy yawning on television when he delivers a eulogy and know he's hardly sincere."

If indeed the experimentalists had much of a case, we would expect the clinics to be glutted with patients suffering from exposure to TV violence. But none of the psychiatrists or clinical psychologists we spoke with reported finding any cases of psychic trauma directly attributed to television violence. Moreover, none of our psychological experts reported finding incidence of such psychic trauma in the scientific journals. There are, of course, constant reports in the literature by the experimentalists, who warn of the great "potential" dangers of television violence. Again, the psychological experts who deal with children every day in their practices have not seen evidence of harm supposedly caused by television aggression.

Is television violence, then, harmful or not?

Replies the noted child psychologist Dr. Louise Ames at Yale University's psychological clinic: "TV violence really doesn't do kids any harm."

Psychiatrist Paul Syracuse elaborates: "Television violence *does* provide a harmless discharge route. Just as a fantasy is a substitute for acting out behavior in reality. I see this every day in my practice. You have to remember that in any kind of situation where an individual's confronted with a reality that is implanted or contains painful elements, he generally has a fantasy that goes along with it . . . or an alternative route that he can use that reduces the tension through the fantasy ending of a story or whatever it might be."

Psychologist Barry Bricklin tells us, "Kids go through violent levels regardless of television exposure where they see explosions and blood and guts all over the place. You see it in their Rorschach tests. Kids have a whole series of defenses to protect themselves from various things. For example, a child watches *Dark Shadows* and is going to be scared. But still he differentiates these TV characters from real-life people. He already knows that television has a long history of lying to him and is not presenting him with accurate facts."

They are also not going to confuse TV violence with violence in reality, says Bricklin. "A person faints in a restaurant and you'll have fifty times the emotional impact because it's *real* . . . and it's right in front of you . . . and you get a sinking feeling in the pit of your stomach when somebody collapses in front of you. Let there be blood, and you'd really flip."

The consensus is it is unlikely children will become inured to violence through TV.

Aren't spy thrillers like *The Man from U.N.C.L.E.* and *Mission Impossible* harmful? They seem so real!

Dr. Irving Markowitz: "Kids become aware of the unreality of television violence. Especially this kind, which is so stylized and exaggerated. The same thing with the comically exaggerated, very flamboyant things on the screen. What you have here are kids impressed with the Superman kind of notion. But, you know, the whole Superman notion in the presence of the immense problems we all have is something we all go in for. 'If I were only Superman and I could fly over all this stuff, then I could do this thing in a different kind of way, and I could escape death!' Most people have all kinds of Superman fantasies. It is one of the commonest fantasies we have. Even in a certain sense the kind of people who say that Superman is God and I will accept God's will. Their belief is that they have a guy fronting for them and they don't have to worry about doing things themselves. '*He'll* do it for me.' This whole thing is built up around man's struggle with his environment."

But surely the cumulative effect of TV violence must be causing psychic damage?

Dr. Markowitz: "I don't believe that TV violence — repetitive or not — is harmful. Violence in life exists. People have to understand this. But they also have to understand that there are resources for coping with it. They must know their *own* resources. With the young people today there is a greater idealism . . . a feeling that people should love one another, feel more for each other. This kind of thing is taking hold with the younger people. Kids may fight each other at times, as they've always done. But, on the whole, I think they have a feeling that brotherhood is a better way of life."

Dr. Syracuse notes: "Many people suspect that constant exposure to TV violence will make them unable to respond to a real situation. That's not true. A real violence situation hits you viscerally. The kids see a real cat struck by a car, tossed by somebody to the side of the road. That's not a cartoon cat. It's a monstrous act . . . they see it . . . they perceive the cruelty and it sickens them. But certainly they don't have *that* kind of reaction to a TV invasion by monsters. It may excite them for the moment, but they see it as a story . . . pure and simple."

If there is no cumulative negative effect of TV, can the medium's cumulative effect offer a positive impact?

"Absolutely," replies Dr. Syracuse. "Children are getting a lot out of repetition because it enables them to master things and they can build up positive learning experiences." Others have pointed out that the factor of repetition helps bring security into the child's life.

Parents reported that their youngsters were most frightened by the news and by such things as TV monsters. However, it is well to keep in mind an admonition from psychologist Barry Bricklin: "The greatest mistake parents make when the kids register some kind of emotional response is to attribute to the child the same emotion they, the parents, have or would be having if they had experienced the same situation as the child. When parents attribute the upset to the child, often what they really mean is that *they* were upset."

Our psychological experts point out that children *like* to be scared, up to a point; it often delights them. What you have to do, as a parent, is make sure the delightful scare does not turn into a fear. This is something the parents of the individual child have to determine for themselves. One youngster's fright threshold is not the same as another's.

As far as instruments of violence are concerned, our experts believe knives are more frightening than guns. Perhaps because of their easy availability, and also because of the castration fear. The more frightening things seem to have some correlation with accessibility. That would probably help explain why some people are easily upset by strangling scenes, even more so by biting. Many people are strong enough to cause strangling. Anybody can bite.

While it is true that children love stories about animals, the reader should understand, too, that a youngster may experience apprehension about a favorite television animal if it appears to be endangered. Some years ago, the young hero on *Lassie* was named Jeff. A youngster we know named Jeff, who was at the time about the age of the television child, had an unusually strong identification with the TV star. The child, as it turned out, also had a dog, and the similarity of life style, dog ownership and name made him overreact very often when either the television child or Lassie appeared headed for danger. So a program that is often thought of by adults as "safe and nonviolent" may turn out to cause occasional fright in a child, requiring the reassurance of his parents.

Should we then conclude, knowing what we now do about television violence, that it should continue running its present course because it is not causing psychic harm to young people? The answer to that is the course of TV violence should be altered drastically. We are not proposing the elimination of violence from the tube, because our feeling is that its dramatization can serve a useful purpose. Granted, there is no need to preserve that kind of dramatic aggression that amounts simply to violence for the sake of violence. But if we are to teach children to deal with violence, an integral part of their lives, it can be done very effectively through television. That will mean that television violence will have to be reconstituted to make it relevant; such violence must clearly be motivational, carefully emphasizing not the body blows but the painful consequences of violence with all its attendant suffering caused the victims of violence.

Dr. Irving Markowitz: "One of the binds you get into with violence on TV is that you keep it remote, but violence has meaning in the lives of kids. And to be brought home to them, it should be part of the drama of their everyday lives. Their own feelings about competition . . . the older brother . . . what goes on in this competition . . . the fights between parents and the kids. That's what has bearing here. But we want to keep it remote from the kids. The answer that parents like to give their kids is that 'It has nothing to do with you.' But it does have something to do with them. Parents are afraid it will contaminate the child by not keeping the violence remote. The victories you win by peaceful methods . . . by collaboration and by discussion . . . give you greater satisfaction in your soul than the victories that are resolved by violence. But you have to show that on television and that is not easy."

Dr. Walter Bromberg is a forensic consultant at Kings County Psychiatric Hospital in Brooklyn, New York. He was a psychiatric witness in the trial of Jack Ruby. Dr. Bromberg says (Walter Bromberg and Gerald George. "Can TV Crime Shows Prevent Violence?" *Today's Health,* May 1969), "Violence is a response to emotional needs, often hidden from view, and occurs when that part of ourselves that demands, 'I want, I hate, I can't tolerate,' breaks through normal controls. Television could demonstrate for the viewer something of the psychology of violence, and nothing else offers such a ready means for preventative education among the public at large." Dr. Bromberg has called on television to present dramas that can make use of the viewer's tendency to identify emotionally with a television character in order to teach people to deal with their own violent natures.

It is, of course, up to the producers of television to follow through and introduce relevance to their violent portrayals. But should the element of relevance be missing, it then becomes the parent's responsibility to provide the element of significance which has been omitted.

There are, nevertheless, certain children who really should not be permitted to watch television at night. The only reason is that it upsets them. It is not a question of their confusing reality and fantasy, but simply because they may happen to be high-strung children. Perhaps they are already churning around with so many things at deep levels that they are confused. Dr. Barry Bricklin offers this suggestion for such children: "Don't worry about sometimes having to set up different rules for different children in the household. Just explain to the child you don't want to watch, 'Look, you just don't handle this too well. It may be unfair, but that's life.' And make sure he doesn't watch."

10 TOO LONG A TRIP: THE TELEVISION ADDICT

How much television is too much? This is not a question that lends itself to a glib response. There are no magic numbers to spell out and delineate what constitutes too much viewing. The problem is less a quantitative one than a qualitative one. What may be too much for one child may not be too much for another. It is not so much a question of time spent but rather a question of the relationship of viewing time to the rest of the activities in a given child's life. Whether there are indeed bad effects from overwatching will depend upon the circumstances, the child, and his environment. To judge whether a child spends an inordinate amount of time before the set demands evaluation of the individual child and the life style to which he has been accustomed. In general there are two very different groups of children who make excessive use of television. The first group includes those who are addicted because it relieves their sense of deprivation, as a narcotic might. The second group finds in the television set a substitute for the things the mother or father does not want to furnish. In the latter case, there is actually an encouragement of television viewing by parents who regard the television set as a cheap and omnipresent baby-sitter.

The television addict by his own choice elects to spend long hours in front of a TV set. This child becomes withdrawn from the world at large, failing to seek friends and direct his interests outward. Seven-year-old Kevin gets up in the morning and before breakfast flips on the television set. He has little to say at breakfast, but keeps his eyes fixed on the tube. Then he is off to school. At lunchtime he is in front of the set again with little to say about anything that went on in school. After school, Kevin is home once more, turning on the television set. He may sit there until bedtime, even having his dinner to the accompaniment of video sound and pictures.

The fact that a child spends many hours watching television should serve as an indicator that there may be something wrong in his life. The problem should be brought to the attention of the family physician.

If overviewing is suspected, parents should have a good look at other aspects of the child's life and examine precisely what is going on. If the child is of school age, one of the first things to determine is whether or not he is doing well enough in his schoolwork. If he has an academic problem, he may be seeking refuge in TV watching.

"A bright kid who is using television as a retreat," says Dr. Markowitz, "a kid who tends to be snippy about his work, may escape to the TV set because there is a certain immaturity about him and he is naïve about the world . . . he is trying to cope with it . . . but to get immunity from the world he becomes a spectator. The way he shows it is by not operating at his full potential. Even if he is getting *B's* in school, he should be getting *A's*. That's because he is too *anxious,* in a sense, to sit down and master his subjects."

Perhaps the youngster is experiencing some kind of difficulty in making or keeping friends. If the suspected TV addict does not sleep well, it should be determined whether that is from too much television watching or because something deeper is bothering the child. Perhaps the child is afraid to go out of the house or does not want to leave the mother's side. He may be watching television as some sort of protection against a very specific excessive fear, say of thunder, and this fear may really be part of a larger phobic problem from which the youngster is seeking protection in heavy television viewing. These are the kinds of things parents must attune themselves to in order to answer the question of whether their child watches TV too much.

It is a comforting but erroneous middle-class belief that the kids who spend endless hours unsupervised in front of the television sets come exclusively from the ghettos. One of the surprising facts we have already discussed is that children in the lower economic brackets watch *less* TV than middle-class youngsters. Many heavy viewing children are abandoned to the television set because their parents feel harassed or too busy to tend to them, but plenty of parents elect to spend most of their free time on the golf course or at the bridge table rather than with their children. A good number of these parents are aware that they are forsaking their kids to the electronic baby-sitter and may even suffer feelings of guilt. Nevertheless, they permit the practice to go on. Many are probably unaware of the implications of not providing adequate TV supervision.

Are there dangers in heavy watching by normal children?

Not in the sense that a normally adjusted child who views too much TV will develop a psychosis. Overviewing, however, can be harmful in another sense. The child, especially the very young one, who looks at television hours on end reinforces his already strong viewing habits. The sheer consumption of valuable time needed in developing a personality is time he will never be able to make up. In that respect, overwatching presents a built-in hazard. As for the parents, allowing too much viewing means they are giving up an opportunity to work with the child in his impressionistic years. They are forfeiting pleasurable years that never return.

Does Heavy Watching Produce Harmful Physical Effects?

There has been some concern that television would cause deleterious physical effects in cases of heavy viewing. One of the fears expressed was that visual impairment might result. In the November 6, 1964, issue of *Time* magazine ("Those Tired Children"), pediatricians at two air force bases reported seeing large groups of children ranging in age from three to twelve who complained of suffering from chronic fatigue, headaches, loss of sleep, upset stomachs, and vomiting. The doctors at both bases were unable to find any medical reasons for the symptoms. After further investigation, they uncovered the fact that these young patients were TV addicts. Heavy viewing for them often peaked to six hours a day during the week and as much as nine hours a day on Saturdays and Sundays. Considering the possible link between television and the physical symptoms, the pediatricians prescribed no television for a period of time.

In instances where the prescription was followed, parents reported that symptoms disappeared as mysteriously as they had begun. Where the prescription was ignored the symptoms remained.

Pediatricians and ophthalmologists we conferred with had never seen patients with these particular symptoms. Some who were familiar with the air force report said they had been on the lookout for such cases but had never seen any. In our survey we did find reports of such physical complaints. Parents said the nausea, headaches and vomiting were not severe or long-lasting but often occurred over the weekends, normally the heaviest viewing days. One reason the symptoms were not seen by physicians may be that they were not considered severe enough for parents to bring to a doctor's attention.

Dr. Markowitz offers a possible explanation for the onset of the mild physical disorders. He says there is a hypnotic effect of the television screen. "If you keep your eyes focused [on the screen] and have trouble seeing it so that you have to stare, you are likely to experience nausea from the hypnotic effect. It is like dangling a chain or watching a windshield wiper. If you watch either one, you can get nauseated. I think this is a matter of mobility or lack of it . . . of moving around or, in effect, of wearing blinders. The kid who looks straight ahead at the TV set, not turning his head to the side, is likely to get nauseated."

Out of all of this one fact has emerged. Even heavy television viewing by TV addicts causes no permanent impairment of eyesight or prolonged physical disability. If you notice your child displaying any of the symptoms we have described, the recommended prescription is to turn off the television set and make sure future viewing time is substantially curtailed.

Temporary Addiction

A child may become a heavy television viewer temporarily because he is in a transitional period in his life. Five-year-old Everett lived in an apartment house where children were not permitted to walk outside in the courtyard. Every time he tried to step outside, the superintendent screamed that he was not permitted to walk on the grass or sidewalks, that it was only for grown-ups. Because of the situation in the apartment house, all of the other parents with children had moved away, so young Everett retreated to the TV set. When he and his own parents moved, the little boy immediately sought out friends and stopped watching television as much as he had been.

Six-year-old Steven moved from South Carolina to New Jersey and left all of his playmates behind. Until he was able to adjust to his surroundings and meet new friends, Steven became a temporary TV addict.

"This transitional period of heavy watching," explains psychiatrist John Spillane, "is not really a problem and causes no harm. You know, dearth of opportunity for meeting friends can be a big obstacle for kids. When they live out in the bush country like Montana, where there aren't many people, the kid may go to the TV set until he finds friends. He may try talking to his mother and father for a time, but you can only talk to your parents so long. The chances are that if a friend comes along he'll just drop the TV habit right there."

Addiction Among Severely Disturbed Children

Based on his clinical experience, Dr. Markowitz is convinced that an already very psychotic child who becomes addicted to television will not automatically become sicker by virtue of his addition to television. "You're talking here about any kind of a focus and whether the focus [television] will make you sicker or serve as a refuge. I think television can act like morphine. The question is: does morphine make you sicker or does it allow you to hide temporarily? In a way, you may say that morphine may prevent psychosis. The same is probably true of television. The patient's symptoms may be worse perhaps if he is allowed to face his trauma without adequate preparation."

There is the great anxiety among many people that TV violence can trigger the emotionally disturbed child to reproduce a behavioral pattern he sees enacted on the screen. Comments Dr. Markowitz: "I don't think this happens. People — and this includes sick people — need to know that there are certain kinds of feelings that they have. I don't think they should constantly repress those feelings or have things shielded from them. I think it's when people try to repress things from them that they're bothered . . . more than when they have to face the truth. Actually, schizophrenic people know what they feel much more than neurotic people. When they watch TV and perhaps see something that strikes home, it's as though the TV set just confronts them with what they already know and says, 'Hey, like so what!' Besides, if they were to see their problem on TV, it makes their problems seem fairly universal . . . so that shouldn't upset them that much."

The triggering mechanisms that may set off a disturbed child to act out some violent behavioral pattern can come from just about anywhere; it is not something that can be pinned on TV. Says Dr. Paul Syracuse in this connection, "I feel that most of the things that set off the borderline kids are from the tremendously disturbing fantasies they have . . . or some kind of emotionally charged incident, say a violent exchange between a mother and father."

The often expressed fear that children will accept false values or stereotypes from television has no basis in fact, *if values and concepts are firmly implanted by the parents or adults in the family.* Our conversations with child development specialists has produced at least one harmonious conclusion: normal, young television viewers, supported by proper supervising techniques, have the emotional and intellectual stamina to resist and override tawdry values and stereotyped images. Misconceptions can be swept away if there is someone around for the child to check with and rely on.

11 LOOKING DOWN ON VIOLENCE FROM THE HILL

In 1954, the attention of the Congress was drawn to the possible effects of television violence on human behavior. The chairman of the Senate subcommittee on juvenile delinquency, the late Senator Estes Kefauver of Tennessee, launched hearings into the matter in response to mounting concern over the increasing number of TV programs containing elements of violence.

Witnesses before the subcommittee often cited instances in which a juvenile who had committed a violent crime suggested that TV violence had somehow been to blame. Stanford University sociologist Wilbur Schramm has pointed out that from his conversations with judges and psychiatrists he has arrived at the conclusion that delinquent children who hold television responsible for their crimes invariably have something seriously wrong with their lives quite apart from television. In the majority of cases, he said, the delinquents have trouble at home — perhaps come from a broken home or have parents who reject them. Schramm said others seem to have psychopathic personalities, with their superegos in a sense disconnected from the rest of their behavioral patterns. Perhaps grossly underestimated at the time of the hearings was the significant testimony of psychiatrist Otto Billig of Vanderbilt University, who told the subcommittee:

"My clinical experience has led me to believe that television programs, movies, etc., have a very limited influence on the child or juvenile. We have performed rather exhaustive psychiatric and psychological studies on juvenile delinquents. Most youngsters do not seem at all influenced by such outside factors. The well-adjusted personality can resist them without difficulties. A very occasional case was triggered into some delinquent act and possibly received specific ideas on how to carry out a crime. But only the emotionally disturbed and insecure individual appears susceptible to such outside forces. Other outside pressures have probably greater significance, such as recognition by neighborhood gangs, inadequate or lack of group activities, etcetera.

"There is little question as to the disturbing educational or artistic value in the poor taste of the mentioned programs, but I would consider it as disadvantageous and even detrimental to the problem of juvenile delinquency to blame them as the actual cause. In so doing we would avoid the main issues. We need to focus our efforts on the principal causative forces rather than on surface efforts on the appearances. Our clinical experience has shown us that insecurities in the individual family play a major part in juvenile delinquency" (from Wilbur Schramm, Jack Lyle and Edwin Parker, *Television in the Lives of Our Children,* Stanford, California, 1961).

During the second session of the 84th Congress, on January 16, 1956, the subcommittee issued its report on the investigation. The conclusions seemed inconclusive, and the members of the subcommittee expressed the opinion that television violence *could* be potentially harmful to young viewers. Beyond the possibility of potential harm existing, no stronger position was indicated by the facts then uncovered in the Kefauver hearings.

Violence Dies Hard

Officials of the three major television networks openly acknowledged to the Senate subcommittee that program routings did wind their way through violent terrain and promised to make changes in content. But checks by the subcommittee in 1961 revealed that the degree of violence in prime time had in fact substantially increased. TV monitoring continued. Then in 1964 the subcommittee, then chaired by Democratic Senator Thomas Dodd of Connecticut, reported that "the extent to which violence and related activities are depicted on television today has not changed substantially from what it was in 1961 and remains greater than it was a decade ago." The subcommittee added that "violence and other antisocial behaviors are, to an overwhelming degree, televised during time periods in which the children's audience is a large one."

In 1964, chairman Dodd held hearings to review what had happened in the three previous years. Said Dodd, "Not only did we fail to see an appreciable reduction of violence in new shows, but we also found that most violent shows of the 1961–1962 season have been syndicated and are now being reshown on independent networks and stations. . . . The outlook is grim. Something must be done. Sociologists, psychologists and other scientists have pointed out . . . that television programs saturated with crime, violence and brutality are dangerous to our children and youth."

For some inexplicable reason the members of the subcommittee, discounting the testimony of clinical psychiatric witnesses, found the evidence gathered by experimental psychologists and TV crime counters apparently more convincing. Dr. Albert Bandura's famous Bobo doll experiment, described in chapter 9, was termed "impressive" by subcommittee chairman Dodd. The Congressmen were also taken with one of the more blatantly inane so-called "aggressive" experiments, involving a large yellow balloon—also described in chapter 9—as an example of how violent behavior is learned. The lawmakers either drew the erroneous conclusion or were led to believe that these examples of learned aggression translated automatically into behavioral violence. While it may be perfectly true that children may learn aggression from television, this learned aggression has shown up in *play situations.* That is the key phrase. The learned aggression in play situations has not been shown to jump the spark gap from the play situation to the social behavior situation. A child may learn aggression, may think about it, may playfully use the aggression, but it does not mean he will then take this knowledge and slug his playmate with a lead pipe.

A noted university psychologist who appeared at the Dodd subcommittee hearings told us, "It is very popular these days to be in the antiviolence school. It gets articles published and they sell. But they have little to do with serving the truth about violence. The Bandura school," the witness charged, "made unfair use of the term 'aggression.'" For example, the balloon experiment referred to by experimental psychologists as "indications of aggression" he termed "completely absurd."

An article in the November 8, 1969, issue of the popular

magazine *TV Guide* quoted some interesting exchanges between the experimental psychology witnesses before the Senate subcommittee on juvenile delinquency and witneses who were television writers or officials. *TV Guide,* showing how debate between the two groups of witnesses nearly always deadlocked, told how the experimental psychologists kept insisting many children up to thirteen years and many adults lacked the capacity to follow TV story lines. This fallacy, which has already been discussed, was meant to encourage acceptance of the theory that counting scenes of TV violence, therefore, represents the only valid procedure of measuring the impact of screen aggression. For instance, Dr. Ralph Garry of Boston University, says *TV Guide,* November 8, 1969, quizzed producer Richard Lewis of Revue Studios as to whether he thought adults grasped the connection between the middle of a western and the end. Lewis insisted normal adults and thirteen-year-olds did understand the connection between the beginning, middle, and end of a play. At this point, the debate came to dead stop.

Later, says *TV Guide,* William T. Orr, a vice president of Warner Brothers, disputed Dr. Garry's contention that eight-year-olds could not understand the plots of the program *Cheyenne* or its moral issues.

"Mr. Orr: Do they understand good from bad, or right from wrong?

"Dr. Garry: They are still in the process of learning it.

"Mr. Orr: The reason I ask the question is that the western is a simple form. The white is usually pretty white and the black pretty black . . . I believe children, even children under six, can understand a simple story of who is right and who is wrong."

Sweeping away the clinical evidence in favor of the experimental, the Dodd subcommittee reported that a relationship had been established between televised crime and violence and antisocial attitudes and behavior among juvenile viewers. "We are greatly impressed by television's achievements in the public areas and by its potential for good in both the education and entertainment fields. Yet it seems clear that television has been functioning as what an informed critic has termed 'a school for violence.' "

Early in 1970 we spoke with Dr. Bandura about his part in the Congressional violence debates. He told us the purpose of his experiments had been widely misunderstood. "They were aimed at determining to what extent a child *learned* about behavior from TV. Most aggressive patterns of behavior are learned without any intent to harm. If one were to test for aggressive or punitive behavior," Bandura said, "an entirely different experimental procedure would have to be devised." He did not tell us, however, *why* his testimony before the Dodd subcommittee was so widely misconstrued and why he had made so little effort to clarify the matter until pressed against the wall by reporters.

The tragic assassinations of Martin Luther King and Robert Kennedy in 1968 impelled the American people to find a suitable suspect to explain why violence stalked the land — the sooner, the better. On June 10, 1968, the suspect was found and indicted. President Lyndon Johnson, staring menacingly at television, charged his newly created National Commission on the Causes and Prevention of Violence with responding to the same, familiar question: "Are the seeds of violence nurtured through the public's airways . . . that reach the family and our young?"

The commission immediately set about the task of holding hearings and chewing the cud left over from the Dodd investigation. At the same time, the blue ribbon group, chaired by Dr. Milton Eisenhower, studied TV programs. It compared *one week of programming in 1967 with the same week in 1968* and purported to give a well-rounded picture of the effects of television aggression. It defined violence as "the overt expression of force intended to hurt or kill"; yet it introduced into evidence Dr. Bandura's by now battered Bobo doll and the thoughts about breaking a yellow balloon as violence. The commission defined as a program "any discrete story unit, from a short cartoon to a full-length movie."

The violence commission spent a good portion of its time counting sequences of aggression shown on the television screen, once again clinging to doubtfully valid procedures laid down by the experimental psychologists. It did, however, point out, and rightly so, that most programs did not portray the *physical and psychological consequences* of violent sequences shown.

On September 23, 1969, the commission issued a tilted statement concluding that violence on television encourages real violence, especially among the poor, disorganized families. Its other findings stated that TV violence may desensitize viewers, making people more willing to engage in aggressive actions in real life when provoking circumstances arise. The commission also suggested that "a steady diet of violent behavior on television has an adverse effect on human character and attitudes." And there was also the astounding conclusion that parental influence may be reduced and counteracted by television, a fact stoutly contradicted by psychiatric experts. The violence commission finally called for further study of the medium to understand its impact more thoroughly.

Accordingly, in March 1969 the chairman of the Senate subcommittee on communications, Democrat John Pastore of Rhode Island, called on HEW Secretary Robert Finch to instruct the Surgeon General to launch yet a new study. The purpose of this latest investigation of television, in the words of the HEW chief, was to "devise techniques and conduct a study . . . using those techniques which will establish scientifically, insofar as possible, what harmful effects, if any, these programs have on children."

The Surgeon General Examines Violence

The National Institute of Mental Health was handed the responsibility of overseeing the functions of the Surgeon General's Scientific Advisory Committee. The Surgeon General was named chairman of the committee; and psychologist Eli A. Rubinstein, Ph.D., assistant director for extramural programs and behavior sciences at NIMH, became vice chairman. Richard A. Moore, special consultant to HEW Secretary Finch, was appointed to serve as the liaison with the committee.

The Scientific Advisory Committee is to feed information to the Surgeon General and to oversee research techniques being developed by the National Institute of Mental Health. NIMH, meanwhile, is also to function as a central clearing house for new research findings from other sources and for inquiries and responses about the committee's work. One of the hopes is that the Surgeon General's group will turn up new knowledge about television's impact on social behavior—and, in particular, its effect on children. To carry out the project the government has set aside approximately a million dollars, not very much money as these studies generally go.

The committee, recognizing that comprehensive answers to questions concerning TV's influence cannot possibly be arrived at over a short span of time, divided its research efforts into two phases. The first phase, research leading to some immediate, practical answers, we can expect to be completed sometime in 1971 or perhaps no later than the end of 1972. The second phase, a long-term comprehensive examination of the medium, will take an indefinite period of time to complete. Invitations were extended to some fifty research organizations and to about a hundred key research scientists throughout the country to participate in the lengthy project. Skeptics express the opinion the Surgeon General's Scientific Advisory Committee will not come up with much more information than previous governmental studies have so far uncovered. Others who voice confidence in the project feel certain new findings will establish whether or not television has a harmful effect on viewers. But, in any case, it is hoped that the committee will refrain from leaning heavily on previous, controversial evidence compiled by experimental psychology and instead approach the problem with a truly fresh viewpoint of objectivity.

12 HERE COME THE JUDGING: WHAT'S GOOD AND WHAT ISN'T

If you are a traveling salesman, and a good one, you have had to learn one significant lesson — you must know the territory. If you are trying to select the best hog in the county, you had better know all parts of a hog. In short, to judge anything you have to know the animal you are dealing with and you have to know the territory.

The Television Animal and How It Romps

Balance and *variety* are two key words in maintaining a semblance of sanity and a measure of satisfaction in this free-swinging world. And *balance* and *variety* are also the words parents should keep in mind in directing their children's television viewing habits.

Many parents complain that one of their objections to television is that their children are subjected to pure pap. It is their feeling that all TV has to offer is pure entertainment, much of it inane and a waste of time. Other parents have told us that they "don't want any of that educational stuff." They say their kids are hit over the head by their teachers five days a week and object to television prolonging the educational pursuit.

It has become something of a tradition to have people draw a line between what they consider an "educational program" and one they label "entertainment." The fact of the matter is that the best kind of children's program has elements of each. There should be a finely woven blend that may be difficult to separate. CBS-TV's *Captain Kangaroo,* for instance, to some represents an "educational" program; to others it is strictly "entertainment." The superior program for children not only captivates the young audience but it leaves them with something to carry away from the tube. Again, *Sesame Street* may be thought of as "educational" by an adult, but to a child it is sheer entertainment.

Our study shows that most children will not be harmed by the range of programs — good and bad — if they are not allowed to spend huge blocks of time viewing. In olden times — before television — kids trudged after their parents to the distant grocery stores and the butcher shops, hung around while mother spent long, arduous hours washing clothes and dishes by hand. Nobody had much free time. But all that has changed, and today grown-ups and kids alike have much more leisure time to fill. So, realistically, we can expect children to fritter away some of their free time, and whether they spend it cutting up papers — hopefully, not Dad's sales receipts — or viewing a few inane cartoons, it will not injure their psyches one bit. Balance again is the watchword, and a little unwinding time may help them relax. The parent, however, should see to it that the viewing does not go on interminably and should direct the child to other activities.

Generally speaking, children can be expected to derive from television a blend of entertainment and intellectual stimulation and at times, under some circumstances, a little bit of emotional warmth and understanding. The stress in the program *Misterogers' Neighborhood* has been on emotional development in youngsters. Referring to that children's show, psychiatrist Paul Syracuse says, "If there is some kind of deprivation going on in the family, Rogers may ease the child's misgiving. After all, kids can form warm relationships with the cop on the corner; why not with a person like Misterogers on the TV set?"

Robert Keeshan, CBS's Captain Kangaroo, believes that television can do much to meet children's emotional needs. "I think it's important," he says. "The whole tone of our program deals with their emotional needs — the quiet pace, for one thing, builds confidence in the character [of the TV personality]. We also have to be aware of the *possibility* of causing stress. I think some of the tried and true formulas of entertainment — the cartoons, the cliff-hangers, the enormous violence we see in some programs — I reject as not valid with children. Sure you can say this didn't affect kids, and some psychologists might agree with the notion that it might even be helpful to them. But there are an enormous number of children we are reaching in this mass medium where this is not healthy. Then somebody will turn around and say this is the parent's responsibility . . . to shield the child. But the child most affected is the one who does not have the parent to shield him . . . does not come from a healthy happy home situation. So I think we have a responsibility . . . we are a mass medium."

We do not share all of the fears expressed with regard to the harmful influence of television. We do not because clinical evidence has failed to establish any direct link between TV violence and violence in the child's behavior. But Captain Kangaroo's view is probably valid with respect to values. In any event, Robert Keeshan believes in not taking chances, and the program reflects his concerns for young people.

Children Two to Six Years Old

The better programs for very young children have host figures who appear warm and gentle. Their personalities should radiate a rapport with the child at home and build trust in the performer. Establishing this relationship is a vital task for the host; it is something children eagerly respond to. Tiny preschoolers are going through the developmental stage where they may worry that those around them may disappear, never to return. So it is not uncommon for the young child to burst into tears and require consolation when the program comes to an end and the host says, "Goodbye until next time." That next time is important to the child who waits impatiently for his television friend to come back again.

Good TV programs for children make use of repetition. We have already shown that the advantages of repetition are that it can reinforce TV learning patterns and that it can allow the child to make correct predictions of what is to appear on the tube next, something that helps the child feel secure.

Humor is an almost essential ingredient in holding a young child's attention. If he is delighted by what he sees, he will sit still for a time and continue watching what is on. Joan Ganz Cooney, director of the Children's Television Workshop (see chapter 13), certainly agrees with this point. "It's pretty low-level, banana peel humor that we often see on TV. I personally can't stand some of our own [*Sesame*

Street] spots . . . for example, the guy who says, 'Two chocolate cream pies' and always falls down the steps. . . . This completely turns me off, but it completely turns the kids on." The important point is that the humor can serve as a vehicle to content.

Comments NBC's vice president of children's programs, George Heinemann, "There is a tendency among some people who produce children's programs to fool around with humor too much. These are the producers who never made it in the adult world. They are frustrated and, as children's producers, they think up funny names and cute little things that the kids don't care about at all. Humor for a child is something that involves him with incongruous situations at *his* level. In other words, when he sees the funniness of a serious situation, which he lives with on an everyday basis . . . and if things are thrown into juxtaposition or contrast to other things, then he sees the humor in that and it involves him. He also gets a great charge in hearing someone else's enjoyment in something."

There has always been a misconception among television producers that a program will hold the child's attention if it is fast-paced. This, of course, is absurd. The child will just as easily watch a slow-paced program that may drive some parents straight up the the wall. Many youngsters feel more comfortable watching low-key personalities like the Friendly Giant, Misterogers, and Captain Kangaroo than program personalities who race on and on. The advantage of the slow pacing is that it allows whatever is presented to seep down slowly. A lot of fast-paced shows may hold attention as long as they are on the air but are often easily dismissed once they end.

"Parents, adults, and children are all held by fast pacing," says George Heinemann. "But that's when there is no motivation or validity to what is being said. The problem is too much fast pacing, no back-up, no real meaning behind it, fast pacing that is only attractive for that split second and that moment, which is a form of escape. So I am not in favor of fast pacing for fast pacing's sake. But I certainly am aware that the mind we serve today comprehends much faster than the mind we served fifteen years ago."

Puppets are frequently used on good children's programs because they are friendly creatures with whom children can easily identify. Some performers find puppets serve quite a functional purpose; it is a lot easier to deal with ten stuffed animals than with ten live actors. There are also performers like Fred Rogers who believe puppets serve a psychological use, too. He thinks the reason kids like them so much is that they are about the only things little children are able to control, and, in the case of hand puppets, when a child plays with a puppet, he puts it on his hand and regards it as a part of himself. In any event, puppets are intriguing for most children to play with and watch on television.

Robert Homme (alias the Friendly Giant) likes to point out that a good children's program attempts to stretch the boredom span. By this, he means the program should help teach children to sit through portions of the program that may not make much sense until the entire show is seen. It is what Homme considers a vital part of the maturing process.

The young child's program should also have very clear simple storylines and avoid complicated plots. Young chil dren are still in the process of making transitions from following isolated TV sequences to comprehending simple storylines. "I think the world is preoccupied with the whole notion of change," says Robert Homme. "But there are a lot of things that had better not change. And one of them is the concept of clarity and coherence." Homme also tells us that it is a good idea for young children's programs to have finality to them. Young preschoolers are often a bit anxious when programs end in a cliff-hanger to be carried on the next day. This is a situation they come to deal with as they grow older. One other essential ingredient of any good children's program is the absence of condescension. The performer who talks down to the kids violates the very basic principles of dealing with children.

Children Six to Nine Years Old

The commercial television networks have not been producing children's programs with the middle range youngster in mind. Not long ago programmers were using the word "children" to include all young people under eighteen without bothering to make much distinction. The only efforts to deal with children between six and nine have been made by public television stations. The success of *Sesame Street* has shaken the commercial networks right in the middle of their children's sections but the Children's Television Workshop again may have to lead the way with a program like *Sesame Street* for the older children.

There is no doubt that this group of youngsters is difficult to program for. The networks until now have used the difficulty as an excuse not even to try. If and when they do, it will undoubtedly be due to outside pressures and competition of public telecasting. The problem of programming for these children is concisely explained by vice president Heinemann of NBC:

"This is a difficult age range to program for because it is transitional. It's when the child is beginning to learn at *his* own rate, and all those rates of learning are different. And, as a result, the child is halfway between the need for very young programming and the need for mature programming. So it's not a clear-cut audience and it isn't easy to find . . . and it isn't easy for the programmer to build programs to suit it.

"The young child is really concerned with the need for life experiences which will help him to relate to older people. He has an intense desire to be like all other people. It may carry over for the rest of his life. But in this period of his life where he's young, he wants to be assimilated into the social group. So he likes life experiences which tell him things that other people do. But the older child likes singular experiences which involve *him*. And let him relive a part of his early life, so he can relate to the experiences he has already had . . . by what he is now seeing and, at the same time, he likes *singular* experiences that involve him. He imagines he is that boy on that horse — whereas the younger child says, 'That is a boy on a horse.' The older boy transfers himself to that horse: 'That is *me* on that horse.' The older child wants that intimate kind of a reaction."

According to George Heinemann, the biggest problems you face in programming for children are not presented by the kids themselves, but by the adults. They are the ones, says Heinemann, who are the most difficult ones to convince when you have a good idea.

"When you get a note from topside saying, 'I hope you have enough money to make the dinosaur move,' as I did when I was producing "The Enormous Egg" (*NBC Children's Theatre*), I had to write a letter back saying, 'Thank you very much, sir, but we have enough money and the dinosaur will not move except in the child's imagination.' The adult thinks the child must have everything spelled out for him. This is the big criticism of the Disney things, where so many adults get into the act, there is no imagination left. The child has no chance to use his imagination. If there is one time in his life when the imagination is the most important and most active, it is when he is from six to nine or ten years of age. That is when he imagines . . . and has no difficulty moving between the real world and the world of imagination. But after that time, all the mores and social pressures . . . and all the rest of the problems set in on him, and he begins to climb into a shell . . . and his imagination begins to disappear."

Children between six to nine are beginning to form the roots of value judgment. It is essential that parents maintain a close contact with their viewing habits and be able to assist them in developing patterns of taste. Says TV critic Judith Crist: "I used to watch with my son when he was between six and eight, and . . . for example . . . we would watch *Gilligan's Island*. I would sit there through the whole thing . . . even though I was almost out of my head. And then I would ask him, 'Well, what did you like and what did you think was so funny?' And this is the only way that parents can give their children a set of values, and this is what parents just have got to do."

13 NEW PASSWORD TO LEARNING: "*SESAME STREET*"

The first time I met Joan Ganz Cooney in her office, I remember looking at her, as she sat across from me on the sofa, and thinking, "Here is a remarkable woman." She is attractive, poised, and full of self-determination. More than that, nobody is going to put anything over on her.

"This country sentimentalizes children more than any other country in the world," she said. "But it's less willing than any other country in the world to put its money where its words are."

That was the way Mrs. Cooney launched into her attack on the plight of children's television.

"What would it take to make preschool TV better?"

"The history of television has been downhill as far as children is concerned. It would take a lot of concern on the part of the networks. And frankly I've just never seen this concern."

Helen of Troy, 1968 — preparing to launch an idea that would spell the ruination of classic television trash for kids.

Learning Begins at Home

In the view of the National Education Association, the need to increase the accessibility of preschool learning experiences is of paramount importance. There are about twelve million children in the nation between three and five years of age. Of that number, perhaps four-fifths of the three- and four-year-olds and a quarter of the five-year-olds do not attend any kind of formal school. It is true that the federal government has tried to provide preschool education for economically disadvantaged youngsters through Head Start programs. But the NEA has argued that all children should be provided the opportunity to go to school at public expense starting at age four. If such a plan were implemented, the estimated costs of providing teachers and facilities even for only four million of those children would approach nearly $3 billion a year. And this does not even include required expenditures for new classrooms to accommodate the youngsters. Let us assume money for this massive educational undertaking were readily available. Still, the years it would take to achieve universal education for four- and five-year-old children would represent wasted time.

The need to reach these very young people is so important because two-thirds of an individual's intellectual development takes place *before* he begins his formal education. Dr. Joseph McVicker Hunt is a professor of psychology at the University of Illinois and one of the thirteen members of the Children's Television Workshop board of advisers. Says Dr. Hunt: "It's important to reach children early because it's during the first four or five years of life that a child's development is most rapid and most subject to modification. During this period, a child acquires the abilities on which his later abilities will be based."

Given these circumstances, it was completely reasonable that some partial solution to the problem be sought, one that would be less expensive and at the same time fairly swift. Television appeared to offer one promising answer. First, because nearly every home in the country has an operating TV set and preschool-aged youngsters are among its most ardent viewers (in fact, more families own television receivers today than have bathtubs, telephones, or subscribe to newspapers). Second, because anybody who has kids knows that they learn readily from television. Accordingly, a consortium of public and private agencies helped establish the Children's Television Workshop to develop and telecast a daily hour-long television program for preschoolers that would simultaneously entertain them and promote their intellectual and cultural development. Among the original financial supporters were the Carnegie Corporation, the Ford Foundation, the U.S. Office of Education, the U.S. Office of Economic Opportunity, and the National Institute of Child Health and Human Development. Several other governmental and private agencies, including the Corporation for Public Broadcasting, the Markle Foundation, and the National Foundation of Arts and Humanities, joined in the venture.

The precise impact of a well-produced TV program on the learning process was not known at the outset. Yet the executive director of the Children's Television Workshop (CTW), Joan Ganz Cooney, pointed to the necessity of not delaying. "We cannot wait for all the answers before we begin," Mrs. Cooney said. "New means must be tried if we are to find solutions to our educational problems." In her original proposal to funding sources prior to the establishment of the workshop, Mrs. Cooney commented, "We propose the creation of a daily, hour-long program for preschool children to be carried nationally on educational and possibly some commercial stations. While the program is intended for all children, the background, problems, and needs of disadvantaged children would be kept uppermost in mind during the planning and promotion of all programs."

In contrast to the $3 billion forecast as needed annually to educate four million children, the estimated cost of a year's development and research for the CTW television program and six months' programming was put at $8 million. While the amount sounds high at first blush, in comparison to $3 billion it is peanuts; added to this is the fact that television could potentially reach the vast majority of young people in the preschool audience and of the two- and three-year-olds as well. "If this country can get a man on the moon," Mrs. Cooney told us, "surely we should be able to figure out how to use this instrument for the betterment of society."

Open Sesame Street

The CTW proposal impressed its potential financial supporters, who concluded that the nation's preschoolers could indeed benefit from television. But the feeling was that the message carried by the medium would have to be carefully remolded and shaped to generate excitement and substantive content. In March 1968 the proposal was accepted, and the Children's Television Workshop was born. The appointment of Mrs. Joan Ganz Cooney as executive director put the vast experimental project in the hands of one of television's most capable executives. Mrs. Cooney had been a prizewinning producer of television documentaries for New York City's educational TV outlet WNDT and, more recently, television consultant to the Carnegie Corporation.

More than a year of research was to be devoted to the development of the now famous program *Sesame Street,* which is seen from coast to coast on both educational and commercial television channels.

Chosen to head the research project itself was Dr. Edward L. Palmer, who had just concluded a study of television viewing behavior among preschoolers while he served as associate research professor in Oregon's State System of Higher Education. Dr. Palmer was one of the few social scientists in the U.S. who had devoted time in the immediate past to studying TV's impact on young children.

In Dr. Palmer's own words, "The *Sesame Street* series represents not one experiment but several. It is an experiment in public broadcasting, preschool instruction, film and television production, formative research and evaluation, and the use of professional audience building techniques. One unusual facet of the experiment is the close working partnership between research and production." By this, Dr. Palmer meant that the findings of his research group were to feed directly into the productions of the telecasts. They were — and still are — subject to constant review, changes and refinement. If certain learning methods are found to work with the children, they are employed; if not, they are discarded.

The question arises why a sum like $8 million has been required to turn out a successful program. Estimated research costs of a half-million dollars rose to nearly three-quarters of a million by early January 1970. One must bear in mind that in the two decades during which TV had become the country's most popular mass medium no network or university had carried out extensive, long-term studies of the impact of television on young children. By the time the program went to air in November 1969, *Sesame Street* was one of the most thoroughly researched, tested, and studied programs in the history of television.

In our research for an article on children's television for the *Atlantic* magazine ("What's Good About Children's TV," August 1969), we confirmed the fact that universities were making scant effort, if any, to determine television impact on the young. We had, for instance, contacted such institutions as Harvard, Stanford, UCLA, Columbia, and New York University to see if any work of this nature was being carried out in the departments of child psychology, psychiatry, education and communications. One or two schools reported they were engaged in film impact studies and claimed these could be equated to impact studies on television itself. We took exception to these claims because we doubted that film impact studies had any direct relationship to daily television programs viewed at home on the TV screen.

CTW, then, was setting up an exploration track from behind the starting gate. It can be expected that the research findings from *Sesame Street* can find application on other, similar educational programs. Undoubtedly, the initial heavy investments to test learning procedures will substantially decrease in cost as more proficiency is gained in the testing and measuring techniques. One of the underlying premises in the production of *Sesame Street* was that the presently accepted animation techniques to which children have become accustomed be adapted to serve an educational function. But animation done well is fiercely expensive—especially since it must have the professional capability of competing with commercial network productions. The mixture of generous strips of fine animation with live professional performers became one of the major items in the program's budget.

As part of the extensive preparations for *Sesame Street,* more than eighty authorities in fields ranging from medicine and child development to film production convened for a series of seminars in the summer of 1968. At these three-day sessions, which were held five times, the experts discussed and suggested educational goals for the project and considered the many production alternatives open to them for the telecasts. According to the workshop officials, those topics of discussion covered such complexities as perception and space conceptualization, language skills and mathematical reasoning. From the many suggestions offered, a set of basic goals emerged. Among them, CTW considers symbolic representation and problem solving of prime importance. Concentration on *Sesame Street,* therefore, is put on rote counting, counting objects, identifying and labeling numerals, and on letter recognition. Underlying constant reference to numbers and letters of the alphabet is the concept that numbers and forms can be symbols that represent objects and events in the real world. Classification, ordering and reasoning skills, part of the basic problem solving techniques present in everyday living, are also featured on the program.

The chairman of CTW's board of advisers and consultants is Dr. Gerald Lesser, Bigelow professor of education and developmental psychology at Harvard. Dr. Lesser says, "Another area of objectives includes showing kids that people can treat one another kindly . . . with a little warmth and courtesy. We're not saying that people always do treat each other with kindness and warmth, but we are trying to create an atmosphere on the show in which that is the general way people are depicted getting along with each other. In addition, we are trying to do a few other things that are less easy to measure in terms of whether we are succeeding or failing. For example, a lot of TV is visually ugly. . . . We are trying to create another option for kids."

Dr. Edward Palmer hates to make broad generalizations about most things. "I guess I'm a typical qualifier," the young, soft-spoken CTW research director told us when we first met. At the time, he happened to be mulling over the report of the violence commission which had just been released. Did Dr. Palmer agree with the findings of the commission? Did he believe children would be adversely affected by TV violence? "I don't think we have all the data necessary to make the judgment," he replied. "For example, to know whether they can recognize types of violence that are there just to move the plot along. . . . When they see *Roadrunner* . . . I doubt if that leaves any effect on the child." What Dr. Palmer believes in are substantiated facts rather than opinion.

Dr. Palmer's research group had just launched into intensive studies to find ways of captivating an audience of preschoolers who were to be taught a specific curriculum. Interviewed midway in the prebroadcast testing period, Dr. Palmer told us, "One of the things we did a lot of research on was the attempt to identify the forms of program that will capture and sustain the attention and interest of young children. We dealt with four-year-olds exclusively . . . assuming that we get little children, you know, from three to five. And we found a number of forms in which interest is generally sustained. We have a very good feel for the program to come as a result of this research."

The findings of Dr. Palmer's group fed — and continue to feed — into the production of the program. For the producers, this coordinated production effort with a research team proves a novel, fruitful experience. Of course, there have been some frustrations along the way for the producers, who frequently needed rapid answers to questions that were not always available, and for the researchers, who could not always provide the required information as rapidly as they would have liked. But in time the cooperative team effort reached such a degree of harmony that producers often preferred discussing the new ideas with the research team before attempting to put them into practice.

Following the basic testing period Dr. Palmer reported that "as a result of our research with young children, we developed several working guidelines for what is most likely to arouse and retain their interest." He summarized some of CTW's findings: "Television material should be lively, full of novelty, have considerable variety, and, as much as possible, use animals, young children, and adults who speak in a friendly and affirming manner. These guidelines, however, are just that; they are neither the last word nor foolproof. We prepared a live-action sequence to explore the concept of rectangles. Theoretically, it had all of the elements to assure success — novelty, variety, fast pace, and general visual sophistication. But it didn't work. It had too much of all of these qualities. As a result, the attention of our preschool audience wandered. There was no evidence they had learned the concept, and, indeed, some seemed confused."

CTW researchers also discovered that young children lose interest if an adult on television talks full-face to them. The problem seems to be that language difficulties are too severe for the preschoolers. Says Dr. Palmer, "They have enormous difficulty in constructing a mental image of a scene from a spoken description. However, we found that interest can be maintained for a longer period if as the adult speaks the camera shows what the person is referring to, such as a pair of shoes, an animal, or a home."

Repetition and *spacing* are also factors that have been thoroughly tested. *Sesame Street* uses repetition to build into each segment of the program several simultaneous levels of learning readiness. This enables three-, four- and five-year-olds to learn something from each viewing. In this instance, repetition ensures the maximum planned effect. The obvious kind of question that spacing presents is this: how often should a one-minute segment (called a *spot* by CTW) be repeated to achieve maximum learning level? Once every day for five days, or perhaps five times a day? This is not a question that can yield an easy response, because it will differ from one spot to another depending upon what kind of information CTW is trying to get across. For example, when CTW tried to teach the letter J it found it more effective to present the J spot five times a day for five days.

One of the key jobs Dr. Palmer's group is responsible for is building test items consistent with objectives of the workshop's curriculum. Another is to devise tests that determine just how effective a completed production segment is. For example, if they want to teach the child the letter H, the research team may ask those children who have viewed a completed H spot to select the letter H from an assortment of line drawings. Then the children may be asked to select the picture of some object that begins with the letter H. It was discovered that a performer's voice and mannerism are extremely important to a youngster. If the quality of the performer's voice or style seems unpleasant, the small viewer may literally or figuratively turn the television guest off.

To test for attention-getting magnetism, the workshop would visit a day care center in New York City. Preschoolers there would be shown a television set that had been tied electronically to a video tape recorder. Sometimes one child would watch at a time. The video tape recorder would then run off on the TV set the latest completed CTW-produced segment to judge the children's reactions. An instrument called a *distractor* was placed next to the set. It was simply a rear screen projector that showed different slides at eight-second intervals. The power of the distractor to capture the child's attention from the TV-produced segment was gauged every eight seconds and charted on a graph. In this way, it was possible to determine exactly which elements of the TV production held attention and which did not. CTW discovered almost immediately that their suspicions had been correct, that cartoons are indeed able to capture and sustain the attention of young children. The researchers also learned that the very young children preferred even simpler visual displays than are generally seen in a typical theatrical cartoon.

"What we found," remarked Dr. Palmer, "is that we can

sustain the level of attention [of youngsters] and still have that televised presentation carrying a full load of instructional content. Some of the things we found that are most exciting to me are the ways of getting across the instructional and entertainment portions together without their competing with each other for the child's attention. We now know we are able to compete with anything the commercial television stations have to offer."

In July 1969, five months prior to telecasting *Sesame Street,* CTW field tested five hour-long experimental versions of the program to judge appeal of the show as well as its instructional effectiveness. The evaluation took place following viewing tests in Philadelphia and New York City. In Philadelphia, two groups of four-year-olds watched the shows individually in their own homes as it was aired over a local educational TV channel. The first group were black children from a disadvantaged neighborhood; the second group was comprised of white children from a middle-class neighborhood. In New York, four-year-olds from day care centers viewed the programs on video tape monitors. These young people looked at the program in groups of varying size. A second day care center in New York viewed *Sesame Street* video tapes under conditions involving deliberate attempted distraction.

After evaluating the results of the tests, CTW found that children who viewed the test programs had exhibited improvement from pre- to post-testing in relation to their respective control groups. When improvement did occur, however, it was not uniform for all goal areas. A number of factors appear to account for the differentiations. For example, the degree of *emphasis* devoted to a given goal;

children generally tended to improve more on those goals that were represented in a greater number of show segments. *Simplicity* was another factor accounting for differences in gains; youngsters showed more improvement in subjects that were presented in a clear and simple manner. Still another determinant was *meaningfulness;* the tests showed children made more improvement on subjects treated in segments that were otherwise judged to be understandable. And *repetition* was found sometimes to be extremely important in goal gains; children sometimes made more overt responses to a program segment that was repeated. In dealing with the letter W, a spot titled "Wanda the Witch" was repeated heavily in the test shows and heavy gains in letter recognition were registered. Interestingly, however, repetition does not always prove effective. The researchers discovered that *the kind of material presented* is often important in determining whether repetition is effective. Certain materials do not necessarily bring much improvement, regardless of the number of times they are repeated, but repetition does work with letter concepts.

The general conclusions showed that, contrary to the view that a child's attention span is too short for an hour-long show, the children tested kept their eyes on the television set between eighty-eight and ninety per cent of the time. The evaluations showed clearly that *Sesame Street* was ready for air. Commented executive producer David Connell: "*Sesame Street* would have been a far different program today if we had not had the research, and it is a far better program because of it."

The first season of *Sesame Street* began on November 10, 1969. During the twenty-six-week run of the shows, CTW's research group continued making in-progress testing of the programs. Again, the main objectives were to make certain that goals of the Children's Television Workshop were being met and that production techniques were modified whenever necessary to make them as effective as possible. Accordingly, after the show went to air, interim checks were made three weeks, six weeks, and three months later. At the completion of the telecasts, an independent evaluation of *Sesame Street* was carried out by the Educational Testing Service at Princeton, New Jersey, to judge the overall impact of the program series on young children. These tests were made in Boston, Philadelphia, Durham, and Phoenix to get a complete, representative nationwide sampling.

A great portion of *Sesame Street*'s success is owed to two of its gifted producers. CTW's executive producer is David D. Connell, formerly the executive producer of CBS's *Captain Kangaroo.* Workshop producer Jon Stone is also a veteran of children's programming on network television; he, too, is a graduate of the *Captain Kangaroo* show. Mrs. Cooney recalls her early conversations with Connell and Stone when the workshop first opened its doors. "I told them to think of our new show as a kind of Rowan and Martin *Laugh-In* for kids . . . because I wanted it to have a very mod look about it. I told them to think of using commercials to sell letters and numbers instead of products, and that's precisely how they've gone about and done the show. Of course, they have brought a great deal more to it . . . I mean those were the bare bone ideas . . . and I would say that virtually nothing has changed from the original conception."

Joan Cooney says she might never have found her exceptional producers had it not been for CBS programming vice president Mike Dann. Shortly after the CTW plan was announced, Dann wrote to her offering aid in finding a top-notch production team. "It is a trick to be able to do five shows a week," he told her. "You're faced with one gigantic problem . . . that of finding the right executive producer." The man Mike Dann recommended was David Connell, and the man Connell recommended to accompany him on this exciting venture was Jon Stone. "Producers Stone and Connell don't take us back to what we wish television was," remarks Joan Cooney. "They are taking television in the Seventies and turning it into a new thing that will be useful to kids."

Just how long you can hold a young child's attention has been a difficult question to ponder. The automatic adult assumption is that it is almost impossible to hold a youngster's attention for a very extended period of time. In getting people's impression of attention span, we received estimates varying from two minutes to an hour. The important fact to keep in mind is that attention span is not an absolute term. It depends on the actual amount of concentration we expect from the child on any given subject. A program like *Sesame Street* is designed to get complete concentration. To accomplish this, we can expect the two- to six-year-olds to pay strict attention up to perhaps seven minutes. That is why CTW researchers consider seven minutes an outside limit. Most of its segments average only two to three minutes in length; however, some are as short as thirty seconds. Then the subject abruptly changes pace and character, and a new segment begins. Changing segments allows them to hold the kids for the full hour. Other programs do not demand quite the degree of concentration and duration of attention span; therefore, they vary accordingly.

Prior to the first telecast, on November 10, 1969, the Children's Television Workshop attempted to erect as many directional signposts to *Sesame Street* as possible. Newspapers and magazines repeatedly carried announcements of the forthcoming program; many of these promotional messages were contributed by the publishers without charge. To reach into the ghetto areas, CTW arranged to have notices inserted in supermarket shopping bags and in mailing pieces from utility companies and put up posters in prominent places such as barbershops and beauty salons. The president of Quaker Oats Company, Robert Stuart, arranged to employ bagstuffers in the Chicago area stores to join in the effort.

Once the program hit the air, the most effective promotional carrier proved to be word of mouth. The commercial television networks, of course, were in a position to aid tremendously in the publicity campaign. But the apparent threat of new competition made them quite reluctant to participate actively. NBC, for instance, did not donate any time to the effort but instead *sold* a half hour on Saturday, November 8, 1969, to the Xerox Corporation for the purpose. But, says Mrs. Joan Cooney, with a little too much kindness, "That, for the networks, is considered a lot of cooperation." She added, "CBS turned us down quite flat. I don't think they wanted to do much. They offered to play a few commercials, however, on their owned and operated stations."

The CBS action may strike us as rather incongruous in contrast to the magnificent cooperation offered CTW by

CBS programming vice president Mike Dann, who personally helped assure the success of the educational TV venture. But networks are not unlike caterpillars in one respect; some segments elect to proceed in one direction, other segments move in opposing directions, and nobody can be quite certain which course of movement will ultimately prevail following all the undulation.

Any parent who has ever watched his child drop a favorite toy or even leave a plate of ice cream to zero in on the television set when he hears the theme of *Sesame Street* need not ask how popular the show is with youngsters. While *Sesame Street* aims to teach four-year-olds, in the main, children as young as eighteen months have been learning to count and identify letters of the alphabet. The first week the program was on the air, our own two-year-old spent most of his day singing about numbers, and a year later he still liked the family to count with him at dinnertime. To get things started, he will think up counting games that require everybody to join in. Preschoolers are busy pointing out triangles, circles, and rectangles wherever they see them; these are all learning products of *Sesame Street*. Still, the purists among the educators frown on the program, saying the kids will not learn much because formal, conventional teaching approaches are not used. But most elementary school teachers are enthralled with *Sesame Street*. Adults have sometimes had as much difficulty tearing themselves away from the TV set as youngsters. Enthusiastic supporting mail keeps pouring into the educational TV stations around the country.

Barbara Walters, co-host of the NBC *Today* show, says

she is so delighted with *Sesame Street* she would watch it even if her child would not. One of the more thought-provoking comments comes from critic Judith Crist: "When I watch *Sesame Street,* I find myself singing along . . . what a W is and all that. . . . It has all the good teaching techniques and it also has all the techniques of commercials. But I'm also scared to death by *Sesame Street.* I think you can take twelve million kids and brainwash them in no time flat. It's quite all right when you're teaching them the alphabet . . . it all depends . . . but you go on from there to teach them certain values . . . this thing has been so researched, it gives me a terrible 'Big Brother' feeling."

The Nielsen Company carried out a special research project for the producers of *Sesame Street* to determine how well the program was being received. Weekly ratings across the nation were made beginning the day of the first telecast, November 10, 1969. There was a two-week hiatus in gathering data, after which ratings were again resumed. During the week of December 22, 1969, meters were not in service; the next week was the Christmas holiday season and not considered representative. In Table 4 are national ratings gathered for the first six weeks *Sesame Street* was on the air.

The ratings for *Sesame Street* are considered very good in light of the following. In urban areas such as New York the program is doing very well. In New York the program is on the air twice a day, once in the morning and again in the afternoon. During the first week, these New York ratings were recorded: morning, 1.3; afternoon, 3.9. At the end of the second week: morning, 1.8; afternoon, 4.0. Ratings have been going up ever since. Later, daily figures in New

TABLE 4. NATIONAL RATINGS OF *Sesame Street,* NOVEMBER 10–DECEMBER 21, 1969

Week	*Rating*	*Average Number of Households Viewing (in thousands)*
November 10–16	1.9	1,110
November 17–23	2.5	1,463
November 24–30 (Thanksgiving week)	1.9	1,110
December 1–7	2.8	1,640
December 8–14	2.5	1,463
December 15–21	2.6	1,520

SOURCE: Nielsen Rating Service.

TABLE 5. NATIONAL RATINGS OF *Sesame Street,** JANUARY 19–MARCH 22, 1970

Week	*Rating*	*Average Number of Households Viewing (in thousands)*
January 19–25	3.8	2,220
January 26–February 1	3.7	2,160
February 2–8	4.1	2,400
February 9–15	3.6	2,110
February 16–22	3.7	2,160
February 23–March 1	3.9	2,280
March 2–8	3.9	2,280
March 9–15	4.1	2,400
March 16–22	3.9	2,280

* Ratings do not reflect Saturday reruns.
SOURCE: Nielsen Rating Service.

York began showing ratings of more than 5.0. For comparison, *Captain Kangaroo* on CBS showed an average rating of 5.0 for the two weeks ending December 7, 1969.

But it should be understood that the CBS lineup of stations across the U.S. is excellent, whereas the lineup of the NET educational stations carrying *Sesame Street* was extremely poor. This poor alignment of stations tends to deflate the *Sesame Street* figures. In addition, since the rating represents the number of households tuned to the program over the total number in the continental U.S., that means there is a lot of air throughout the country not even carrying *Sesame Street.* That situation is to change with interconnection of the PBS educational network. On the basis of poor station alignment alone, the ratings for *Sesame Street* when the program first aired must be considered to have been very good. In Table 5 are national Nielsen rating figures for *Sesame Street* gathered during the nine-week period between January 19, 1970, and March 22, 1970. As will be noted, the viewing trend continued to curve upward.

Ironically, the extraordinary reception of *Sesame Street* has posed a threat to a number of established children's programs. In a number of television markets, New York included, program managers have committed themselves to aiding in the *Sesame Street* educational experiment. But in so doing, they have bumped older programs to make room, and the result has been a loss of exceptional TV experiences that numerically had more limited appeal. Perhaps more careful planning can provide sufficient space in the programming schedule for *Sesame Street* as well as the programs it unintentionally rivals.

On Beyond Zebra

The second season of *Sesame Street* was again funded by the U.S. government, the Carnegie Foundation, the Ford

Foundation and a number of other smaller grants. The curriculum was expanded to include more complex symbolic reasoning.

The workshop was buoyed by two independent research findings in the fall of 1970. Each survey revealed that *Sesame Street* was assuredly yielding positive results. The public opinion polling firm of Daniel Yankelovich provided an in-depth examination of five hundred families in New York's low-income area of Bedford-Stuyvesant. The study showed that the program achieved almost total saturation. Yankelovich reported *Sesame Street* had reached ninety per cent of the youngsters between two and five and that sixty per cent of those same children watched the program regularly at least once a day and often twice.

The Educational Testing Service of Princeton, New Jersey, furnished the second set of impressive results. Approximately 940 youngsters were selected for testing in five separate regions of the country: Boston, Philadelphia, Durham, Phoenix, and a rural area in the northeastern portion of California. The children in each group were tested prior to viewing the first season of *Sesame Street,* then again later after the season had ended. Included in the sampling were representative youngsters from suburban sections and rural sections, disadvantaged English-speaking children from the inner city and disadvantaged Spanish-speaking youngsters from the urban centers. ETS concluded that youngsters who watched *Sesame Street* most absorbed the most. Children who viewed the program showed greater gains in learning than those who did not. This was true of children in all of the tested groups. ETS found that the skills that received most time and attention on the program were in the main the skills best learned. Disadvantaged children who viewed *Sesame Street* frequently made gains surpassing those of middle-class children who watched the program infrequently. And ETS also found that three-year-olds made greater gains than the older children. This last finding was considered significant because it suggests that three-year-olds are capable of learning many skills traditionally withheld from the teaching curriculum until later ages. In addition, ETS results appear to imply that *Sesame Street* may be quite effective in teaching some skills to children whose first language is not English and who do not test well or perform well in the formal school setting. Concludes Dr. Samuel Ball, the man who directed the ETS research program: "I think we've shown in this evaluation of *Sesame Street* that television can have a profound effect upon the learning of three- through five-year-old children from widely diverse backgrounds, including a strong and positive effect on disadvantaged children."

In July 1970 a new vice presidential name was added to CTW's executive chart. In a move that surprised many, CBS vice president Mike Dann suddenly resigned to accept a post with the Children's Television Workshop. Hardly a step down in Dann's view despite a drastic salary cut, the post represented a new challenge. No longer chafing under the rating game, Dann could now devote his full energies to building the workshop into a powerful force within public television. Dann later said he had grown progressively disenchanted with life at the commercial networks. When, in the spring of 1970, CBS Television president Robert Wood announced cancellation of specials, including the *Children's Hour* and the *Children's Film Festival,* Dann began to conceive of commercial television as a moribund dinosaur. His assignment included developing foreign language versions of workshop productions and supervising acquisition of possible future cable TV channels for CTW. The workshop would never accept the premise that dubbed versions of *Sesame Street* were acceptable for export. Varying cultural and social differences dictated completely distinct productions in order to have maximum impact on children in each foreign environment. Yet one of the most intriguing ideas generated by the workshop staff was the possibility of establishing an entire children's network interconnected via cable television. Such a network conceivably could provide programming exclusively for children all day long.

In his new role, Dann began to thrive with the dynamism of his former network days. By summer's end, the workshop would be able to boast of *Sesame Street* exportations to some twenty-six countries. And by year's end 1971 CTW's goal was to have foreign language versions of the program in Europe, Africa, Latin America, the Caribbean, Australia, New Zealand and much of the Far East. Programs produced in foreign languages were to be recast versions of the English model. All were to be locally produced with local casts, and the hope was that eventually the shows would be financially self-liquidating.

Toward the middle of the first *Sesame Street* season, promising results led the workshop to consider programming for older children. A feasibility study similar to the one preceding production of *Sesame Street* suggested it would be possible to teach children between seven and ten who had experienced some form of reading failure. The object of such a program was to stimulate an interest in the printed word. This project was handed over to producer Samuel Gibbon to carry out. While the reading oriented program for the older youngsters followed research, testing and production patterns similar to those used in *Sesame Street,* the research and testing phase was carried out by one set of teams at the same time that production techniques were experimented upon by other teams. In effect, the new project was telescoped into only a year to make possible a final program target air date of October 1971. Unlike *Sesame Street,* the newest CTW program was also to be accompanied by a good deal more of supportive material, including books and records. This motivated the workshop to look to the organization of an in-house publishing and publicity group that could accommodate such objectives. Thus, the momentum of *Sesame Street* was energized into more and more productive channels.

Some network officials' predictions that *Sesame Street* would surely have a short run after opening night proved catastrophically incorrect. In no time at all, the competition for attracting young viewers to the TV screen found these same executives reshuffling their administrative staffs to recapture an audience lost to — of all things — educational television! Probably the biggest admission came from ABC, which has spoken in curious terms of producing a program called *Curiosity Shop.* It is to be, says ABC, like *Sesame Street* in concept.

14 THE CARTOON CAPER: DO CELLULOID TIGERS BITE HARD?

There they sit on an electronic safari — magnetized to the very edges of their chairs, clicking off the frames that flow by. The television tiger watchers! Armed with double-barreled clipboards, they take careful aim on every aggressive move a cartoon animal takes. They note an animated cat taking a swing at the tiny cartoon mouse. Then, after the cat catches his foot in a mouse trap, the team of watchers grimace in unison and add another tick mark to the growing violence column they are compiling.

Throughout all this business, the kids have been rocking with laughter — an even more sinister sign to the tiger people that the celluloid species do indeed have strong cavity-free teeth that are leaving indelible indentations on the tiny viewing minds.

This undiluted search for the causes of violence has reached a peak of hysteria. The assassinations and social turmoil of the Sixties and now the Seventies has goaded us to look for root causes under our rugs, behind the doors, under the stairs, and finally in the motivation within cartoons. With each of the recurrent acts of aggression of national importance there has been renewed effort to track down the seeds of violence. Each time the job is handed over to a government task force because three things are accomplished: it takes the immediate heat off the politicians and the bite off the public conscience, and whatever conclusions the commission comes up with take on the aura of truth. Nobody feels the sting until the next aggressive act comes along, and a new government task force is assembled to hand down another authentic-sounding pronouncement.

In 1969, the Eisenhower task force reported its experience counting violent episodes on television and listening to the reports of the "experts." The commission's Mosaic pronouncement included a warning to broadcasters to cut out all those harmful cartoons, the ones containing "serious, non-comic violence." We are, of course, left to wonder what is meant by a "serious, noncomic" cartoon sequence.

The Eisenhower violence commission failed to uncover any new principles that will be remembered in the halls of science. But it waved its blue ribbon around enough to lend credence to its results. Many people swallowed those results whole, and several authors even used them to support their own hysterical theses on the causes of violence. But the probe did expose a few raw nerves at the networks, and that was to have an impact on the 1969–1970 programming, especially during the Saturday morning cartoon strip—which some people then called "mayhem in the ayem." CBS and NBC stated publicly that they were responding to the antiviolence passions but continued privately to express the belief that animated violence left no traces of psychic harm.

Thus, CBS vice president Mike Dann remarked to us shortly before the onset of 1970, "There's been a massive change [in cartoons] this year. In the last year, the change in the themes for cartoons is not to be believed. Successful shows have been completely abandoned. High circulation success . . . high profit centers . . . all abandoned because it was a question of violence or because they were too melodramatic."

Many of the cartoons in the season 1969–1970 seem to have eliminated violence to this extent: they eliminated the moment of impact. Bugs Bunny is falling off a cliff, for instance. You follow him down the cliff, but you do not see Bugs hitting the ground, you see perhaps the top of the cliff shaking as you hear the thud.

NBC's Larry White takes credit for much of the "new violent look." Comments White: "You see us here at NBC in a transitional period from I'll say old-fashioned shows to what's new. And we're in the middle of a big change. We're leading the change. We're much further ahead in change than the other two networks. But the other networks are seeing the change possibilities, too, and are beginning to change. We have more foresight, that's all."

Among the interesting things Mr. White announced in February was that he was dropping the *Banana Splits,* a live-and-cartoon mixture program he said had "expanded the areas of fantasy and imagination" and had proved to be "quite a success."

ABC's programming official, Martin Starger, quoted in an article by Terrence O'Flaherty ("Murder on Saturday Morning," *McCall's,* September 1969, p. 142), said: "It would be wrong to say that we're changing our Saturday morning schedules because of violence. Frankly, we're changing them because we weren't doing particularly well with them last season. We have some exciting new shows for children which also happen to be less violent."

Television critic Jack Gould took all of these network

actions in stride, saying, "All they have done, as you must have noticed, is take away the direct physical violence. Instead of it, they have the airplane crashing, which gives the element of violence without getting Pastore irked. But they are very proud of it. CBS is particularly proud. CBS has moved way ahead of this year (1969–1970). It's just one of those things that is lucky, and part good scheduling." We asked Gould if he did not want to give the networks a few points for better Saturday programs this year than last. "No," he replied. "I think it's just an appeasement of Pastore . . . which began over a year ago when the contracts were running out."

Hanna-Barbera, the major source of network cartoon shows, came up with what executive producer Joseph Barbera calls "fun violence." With a bright public relations eye focused on the report of the Eisenhower violence commission, Barbera said, "A cat chasing a mouse is *comically violent.*" This, of course, is in line with recommendations of the commission, which advocated elimination of all cartoon programs containing "serious, noncomic" elements, whatever that means. Barbera warns that from a purely business standpoint, "We cannot eliminate too much of the action, because we're losing our viewers." Then accidentally picking up a psychological finding, Barbera added, "If the cat rams into a wall while chasing the mouse and shatters into a million pieces, the fantasy of animation quickly restores the feline and the cat and mouse game continues. No one really gets hurt."

The idea is that the networks no longer show the moment of impact on the wall. That is something the kids will have to wait and see on the independent stations where all the network syndicated reruns are still playing. So if there really were psychological harm caused by cartoon violence — which is fortunately not the case — it would continue to be seen. Even if the networks were to purge themselves of all violence, that would still leave the independent local stations as free and unencumbered to show the old shows.

The consensus of our child development experts is that cartoon violence can be ruled out as a source of concern for parents. Expressing the unanimous viewpoint is psychiatrist Paul Syracuse: "Cartoons offer an easily accessible discharge route for aggressive feelings. The idea of a small guy outwitting the larger one is perhaps more important to the child than the violence portion of the cartoons. It would certainly fit in with the fantasies, too, because a little child very frequently would like to see himself as a big kid who is throwing the pie in mother's or father's face. I think that this is also a way of reducing the tensions. The humor and the laughter that goes along with the kids watching the cartoons is a tension-reducing mechanism." Dr. Syracuse does not feel that cartoons are too fast-paced to provide meaningful fantasy, either. He says, "You have to remember that the fantasy life of a child moves very, very quickly. I think, in fact, it is so hard to get kids' attention many times because they are fantasizing so much." Dr. John Spillane says that when you talk about violence you have to take into consideration that one of the things that frightens kids is an apparent proximity to the violence. "With cartoons," the psychiatrist tells us, "the kids are completely aware they are dealing with a cartoonland, which is a kind of never, never land . . . and so it doesn't begin to touch them."

The competition for capturing bigger shares of the TV

cartoon business depends largely on how many laughs a producer can squeeze into a foot of film. From the animator's standpoint, the networks are a demanding group. They keep insisting on newer and newer cartoon heroes but seem unwilling to shell out the needed dollars. From the network's point of view, the medium gobbles up the cartoon fare like so many hungry tapeworms. And they believe that the kids will gravitate toward what is new, casting aside favorite shows they came to love the season before. The networks are constantly feeling the economic pinch of their budget departments. So the pressure on the animators is for new heroes and speed in production, and insistence that contracted animations be completed on specified dates. But as far as the animators are concerned, they say they at least are hardly ever pestered by the networks for really fresh material. Freshness, accuracy and aptness of thought went out with the last Jack Armstrong radio serial contest.

Instead of developing new adventures for the heroes of last season's show, animators bring back secondary characters the following season as heroes of new shows. These characters become embroiled in completely unrelated adventures; their new roles have absolutely nothing to do with those portrayed the previous season. Meanwhile, they are playing last season's animated parts in syndicated form on local stations.

In the 1968–1969 TV season, Penelope Pitstop was just another racing driver on the CBS hit cartoon show *Wacky Races;* so were Dastardly and Muttley. But in the season of 1969–1970, Penelope took a lead in her own cartoon show on CBS, while Dastardly and Muttley starred in their own new animated series on NBC. Yet at the same time, Penelope, Dastardly and Muttley kept right on racing on reruns of the *Wacky Races* on CBS, all of which sounds slightly confusing if you are not a cartoon aficionado. If the cartoon animators are really in a creative bind, they can always resort to corrupting some handy classic. Take the *Adventures of Gulliver* (ABC), for instance. If you suspect there is some remote connection between that show and the book *Gulliver's Travels,* you may rest assured even Jonathan Swift would never find it. Jules Verne would undoubtedly have flipped over ABC's corrupted title, "Around the World in Seventy-nine Days," for a portion of their cartoon series *Chattanooga Cat.* These so-called classic adaptations amount only to borrowing a title (frequently distorted), dropping the charm and essence of the original story and leaving simply an excuse for action and chase sequences. Looking at some of these TV "classics" may be one reason some people are discouraged from reading the original.

The cartoons capitalize on anything currently popular. One of the favorite courses for animationists is to take some handy fad and weave it into the story outline. For instance, many cartoons on the 1969–1970 program schedule are reminiscent of the car in the movie *Chitty Chitty Bang Bang.* Dastardly and Muttley may also owe something to Huntley and Brinkley as well as to Snoopy and the Red Baron. Another fad taken liberal advantage of in the 1969–1970 season was the current fascination with the occult, astrology, and witch lore. At night, *Bewitched* and *I Dream of Jeannie* brought in the adult numbers, so the networks tried the witchcraft formula on the kids in the daytime. That is how Sabrina the witch came to be born.

Our impression of many of these so-called new animated

series is that they are spliced-together leftovers, film clips from old shows, as in the case of *Wacky Races.* It is a practice that saves inspiration, spares creative thought and, just incidentally, saves scoopfuls of money. Other reaction to the antiviolence sentiment during the 1969–1970 season led the networks to embrace what has been referred to as "gentle fantasy." Borrowing is, naturally, easier than reflecting on new ideas, so several of the shows looked for inspiration to the Land of Oz. Depatie Freling Studios, another major TV animation firm, for example, gave NBC *Here Come the Grump* — title courtesy of *Laugh-In,* setting courtesy of Oz. The Grump is a dwarf-like creature who rides a goofy-looking dragon. For some unexplained reason, the Grump is forever chasing a boy and a girl. Presumably, the reason for the chase is that there is a lot of film that has to get used up.

Another Oz-type character was NBC's *H. R. Pufnstuf.* He looked to us like a swollen gumdrop, but we learned from programmer Larry White that Pufnstuf was actually a friendly dragon and the mayor of Living Island. "The people of this island," White explained, "are animals, trees, houses . . . they talk, walk, have conversations. When you walk into a library, the books talk . . . they say 'Take me and I'll tell you so and so.' It's the story of a little boy who gets stranded on this island, and he tries to get back with the help of a magic flute and the mayor. But the boy is constantly foiled by a witch, whose name, Witchie Poo, gives an indication of the tone of the show." Commented Jack Gould: "I thought they had a good idea, but it got too confusing because there was just action, action, action, for the sake of having something going on."

Drama may often call for the willing suspension of disbelief; cartoons, on the other hand, for the willing suspension of logic. That is why cause and effect in the latter may not even be distant relatives. What many of us seem to enjoy most about cartoons are the abundance of puns. *Bullwinkle,* for example, is a thoroughly delightful cartoon for grown-ups. Yet the presumption is that kids love the puns just about as much as we do. In tests conducted prior to the première of *Sesame Street,* however, researchers discovered that the puns were soaring straight over the heads of the children. The producers of the program had planned to do a series within *Sesame Street* called "The Man from Alphabet." This was to be a little mystery story with a lot of put-on. But the series turned out to be a massive failure because while the adults were roaring over it, the kids did not even snicker. Again, during the 1969–1970 TV season ABC's *George of the Jungle* made a huge success with adult viewers. Here were some sample lines from one show:

FIRST CHARACTER: "I'm biding my time."

SECOND CHARACTER: "Oh, really! I'm biting my nails."

The puns may not go over with the kids, but the TV station managers seem to eat them up. And, after all, who buys the cartoons?

The costs per half hour of a typical cartoon show range between $6,000 and $10,000. These costs apply to only the typical, average Saturday morning cartoon programs, not to specials which cost a great deal more. The factor that sets the actual figure is largely the quality of the artwork, which includes the form of animation. In general, the more portions of the animated figures that move, the higher the costs. *Full animation* might include movement of facial expressions and body movements in great detail. Such animation is common in the Disney programs. The mass production efforts required by Saturday morning cartoon shows, however, has impelled animationists to hold the line on rising costs. They have had to do this by resorting to a technique referred to as *limited animation.* In full animation, the entire figure — from head to toes — may shiver, let us say. If that shivering effect were to be produced on a Saturday morning cartoon, only a few parts of the body would shake. To produce the full effect may require as many as sixty-four drawings, requiring the artist to work perhaps two days. The limited animation method for television may use only four drawings, a job that could be done in an hour's time. The tremendous saving in costs is not hard to imagine. The great bulk of ABC's cartoons in 1969–1970 were so limited the figures were only outlines resembling comic strip figures whose mouths moved. When the figures were required to walk from place to place, action was obviously stilted and jerky. The choppy, cheap look in cartoons proved to be extremely irritating to watch, especially when the story was meant to be realistic in nature, as in adventure series plots. This is not to imply, though, that just because a great deal of money is poured into a cartoon product it will guarantee aesthetic quality. NBC's two leading programs in the 1969–1970 season, *H. R. Pufnstuf* and *Banana Splits,* largely underwritten by Kellogg advertising, were by the network's own admission "ridiculously expensive" (each show reputedly $156,000). Yet, aesthetically, they were semianimated monstrosities.

Sesame Street's Joan Cooney says, "The only thing that bothers me at all about the Saturday cartoons is the junky quality of the artwork. The violence isn't going to hurt the kids' psyches . . . children know cartoons are a put-on. But what is it doing to their taste! The level of artwork is just awful . . . and we're going to bring up a generation of people who are conditioned to like terrible artwork."

Networks and advertisers take advantage of the confusion between reality and fantasy concepts of the younger kids by deliberately adding to the confusion. At commercial time, it would be a simple matter to fade to black to show a clear break between program and commercial. But one device used more and more these days is to make a direct cut from the last frame of the cartoon show to the first frame of the commercial showing a cartoon figure. It is done in rapid clips to drag you right into the commercial. Promotional announcements for upcoming Walt Disney productions on TV use the device well. Before you realize it, you have been swept right up into the promotion in the most artfully deceptive way possible.

Even an adult can become prey to the device. During *Dastardly and Muttley* (January 3, 1969) the last frames had the pigeon constantly chased by Dastardly and Muttley. Suddenly the lure disappeared from view. Then without any transition, Dastardly appeared on the screen with a Kellogg commercial and it took several seconds for adults to realize the last sequence was not part of the program. Of course, it is an effective selling technique. But it takes advantage of the young viewer nevertheless.

In late 1969, a toymaker (Topper Corporation) filed a complaint with the FCC against a second toy manufacturer (Mattel, Incorporated) for unfair advertising practices. The allegation charged that Mattel had obtained what was tantamount to a thirty-minute commercial on ABC in the following manner. Mattel sells a racing car called Hot Wheels. Topper said the producer of a Saturday morning show obtained from Mattel permission to use the name Hot Wheels as the name of the program. Mattel in turn agreed to purchase a number of commercial spots on the program, although the commercials did not advertise the Hot Wheels racing toy. Nevertheless, Topper considered the identity of the toy and program names so close as to constitute a commercial lasting thirty minutes, the length of the show. In February 1970 the FCC said it was taking steps to order ABC to log as commercial time more than just the three minutes of commercial time purchased by the toymaker, Mattel.

If the FCC action is finally to be carried out, it could have ramifications for the broadcast industry. The assumption is that the FCC will then ask to take a closer look at how many times commercials fall within the confines of program material, and the result could be the commission's formulating new industry-wide rules for commercial logging. The FCC said it found "disturbing" the devious way in which the program had reached television.

A Tour Through a Typical Fun Factory

Hanna-Barbera is certainly a major producer of the Saturday morning cartoon strip. In one promotional piece of copy, these animators boast of a fifty per cent share of the programming. But they tell us that is based on shows lasting from 8 A.M to noon. The network shows go beyond noon, though. We suppose you can get so used to drawing funny figures it is natural some will escape into the promotional material.

Hanna-Barbera supplies all three major networks with programs and it can get to be a tough job, we are told, competing against yourself. Each of the three networks expects the same supplier to deliver it a winner, a rather awkward position for the supplier to be in. Hanna-Barbera's production of the *Banana Splits* for NBC was the top-rated show in 1968–1969, lost out to its own production of *Scooby-Doo* the following season for CBS. The question of how the animationists try to assure originality naturally comes to mind. Hanna-Barbera offered this response:

"This presents a challenging situation each year. We have always been able to develop new concepts for each season. On an average, we come up with about thirty new series ideas for presentation to the three networks each season. Often we will combine two or more ideas to create an entirely new show. Coming up with these ideas keeps the lights burning late into the evening at the studio. We depend heavily on our staff writers to develop new concepts. And, thankfully, together we are able to polish our ideas into salable packages."

We asked Hanna-Barbera whether they used child guidance experts for help.

"Child guidance experts are not entertainment experts. We entertain youngsters, not guide them. Child guidance experts, in many instances, are persons who advocate such film shows as 'A Day at the Public Library' and so forth. These shows are applauded by everyone and watched by no one."

Would Hanna-Barbera consider it better to offer more substantive content to cartoons rather than figures in endless chase sequences?

"Hanna-Barbera is able to produce the highest quality and most entertaining cartoon series seen on Saturday mornings. We are able to accomplish this because we know the business and we know what entertains youngsters. We produce hits for the price the webs [networks] are willing to pay."

A Little Perspective with Cartoons

We believe children are entitled to a few moments of escape, just as adults are, but at some point parents must begin drawing lines. NBC's vice president Heinemann, in charge of children's programming, puts it clearly. "I'm a total supporter of a child having a few moments of escape. You send a child to school five days a week; the teachers beat him over the head and tell him you gotta do this, you gotta do that. My boss says the same thing to me all week. Then he gives me Saturday and Sunday off to relax and recover. Now the child should have the same privilege. The problem is it is too easy for the networks to get an audience . . . and there is too much of it [cartoon programming]. Now the answer is and has always been *balance*. Balance in everything . . . sex, booze, women, church . . . anything! And when you get overbalanced, that's when you run into trouble."

Saturday morning programming has lacked resourcefulness and diversity and is largely bereft of substance. But even if this were not true, even if by some miracle on Sixth Avenue the Saturday morning block blossomed into one admirable program after another, they would not provide a substitute for real life experience. After an hour or two of escapism, the electronic form of unwinding lapses into a pure waste of time; idleness that can and should be put to constructive use. The child must be encouraged to turn the set off after a while and find more useful things to do — go outside and play, find some paper and draw something, take a stroll — whatever. If he does not, the parent must make sure the set is turned off and divert the child's attention to a more constructive activity. It is fine to escape, but then you have to learn to escape from escape.

TV critic Jack Gould offers one final note for tall people: "The adult who sticks out the five hours watching cartoons is entitled to one Bloody Mary for every commercial break."

15 AIR FARE: SOMETIMES A BARGAIN

Television programs frequently have the lifetime of smoke. But a number of them have managed to survive either because they are genuinely good or because of reasons bordering on the occult. In the latter case, as Harvard's professor Gerald Lesser has observed, if you dig down deep enough you are bound to find an economic reason.

In this chapter, we will discuss some of the programs that have achieved a degree of longevity and some that have a good deal of merit.

PRESCHOOL TELEVISION

Captain Kangaroo (CBS, Monday through Friday)

Up to the time of this writing, *Captain Kangaroo* remains the only daily commercial network program for preschoolers, or for children of any age group, on the airways. Its durability is owed primarily to Robert Keeshan, who is Captain Kangaroo. Keeshan, a pioneer in television for children, has managed to guide the show for fifteen years, during which time it often faced choppy competitive seas. The captain's wig for years gave him a comic appearance, but in these days of unique hair styles Captain Kangaroo comes off with quite the mod look. Something of a bumbler to the adults, he always manages to get tricked out of a handful of carrots by Bunny Rabbit. In real life, Keeshan is a sensitive, bright man who is dedicated to children and who knows them well. But it is difficult for most adults to find out very much about him because he is shelled in by a well-heeled office entourage and a public relations firm that give him the aura of the Howard Hughes of the children's world. Trying to reach him is as easy as interviewing a recently returned astronaut locked in the lunar receiving laboratory. It is to Keeshan's credit that he has grown in maturity and stature since his earlier days as Clarabelle the Clown in the old *Howdy Doody* shows. More than that, his knowledge of kids has been derived from instinct rather than from any sort of formal training in child development. Robert Keeshan was among the earliest men in children's television to recognize that entertainment and education are each at their best when they overlap.

The *Captain Kangaroo* program is built around a solid *relationship* between Keeshan and the kids at home. There is never the slightest trace of condescension. The interaction between the performers (Captain Kangaroo, Mr. Greenjeans and Mr. Baxter) is relaxed, yet the overall pace of other program elements is varied and lively. Dropping by during the hour are an assortment of animals, big and small. Some are live, some are hand puppets, several talk, while still others, like Dancing Bear, simply step about with just a little less grace than Gene Kelly.

Captain Kangaroo continues to be one of the most imaginative programs for young people. Yet an occasional detractor will remark the show is "too stereotyped," a comment that ignores the changeover of audiences with succeeding generations.

Keeshan insists on screening his commercials himself to ensure that they are done in good taste. He would prefer charging advertisers a little more for less commercial interruption in program continuity. And he will not permit toys of violence to be shown on the program. Despite the fact that some people object to Keeshan's selling at all on the program, it is a seemingly reasonable price to pay for his being carried by a commercial network for three generations of preschoolers.

Misterogers' Neighborhood (PBS, Monday through Friday)

Happiness, according to Fred Rogers, is resolving conflict. And when he drops by on weekday afternoons to spend a half hour with his friends, the very young, his concern is their happiness and helping them to resolve many of their gnawing inner problems. Comments Joan Cooney, "Friends of mine says that by around five in the afternoon, their kids are cranky and Fred Rogers has a way of soothing them. You might say he's their cocktail in the afternoon." Rogers's child magnetism for years raged on quietly over educational stations like a hidden mine fire. Occasionally, some of the underground smoke found its way into small blurbs in newspapers or into more esoteric publications. Suddenly, Rogers's popularity exploded right out into the open and his *Neighborhood* became visible in major newspapers and in popular magazines. In January 1970 the Corporation for Public TV, a federally chartered group that disburses funds for public TV, gave *Misterogers' Neighborhood* an additional half million dollars. The award will enable 64 more educational outlets to carry the show. That means Fred Rogers can now be seen over 197 stations, virtually the entire lineup of public TV outlets in the U.S.

On the program, Misterogers wears no costume and plays no role other than the one he assumes in real life. During the actual scripting, he collaborates in a sort of creative psychological brainstorm session with Dr. Margaret McFarland, the administrative director of the Arsenal Family and Children Center in Pittsburgh, a division of the University of Pittsburgh's medical school.

In helping children deal with their emotions, sometimes Rogers will discuss anger and love with them. *Discuss* is quite the correct word, because his talks are so personal they frequently trigger a by-play in which the child may respond vocally to a question and Rogers, anticipating the reply, may follow through to his next point. A Boston mother told us she once overheard her young daughter talking back to the TV set. "Misterogers! Misterogers!" shouted five-year-old Claudia. Then she ran into the next room and said, "Mommy, I want to go see Misterogers, *the real Misterogers!* I want to tell him I started school today!" The little girl wanted to communicate with the one person on television she felt would be interested in hearing from her. Mothers who discover the *Neighborhood* program often remark that Rogers helps them to understand vividly just what is happening to their children through the different stages of their development.

Quite often Rogers will deal with fears, real or imagined. During the 1969 fall season, *Misterogers* devoted an hour-long special to the subject of childhood fears and fantasies when the lights go out.

Every weekday children are escorted aboard a unique trolley that transports them to the Neighborhood of Make-believe. There they find a group of puppets and people in a fantasy land presided over by King Friday the Thirteenth and Queen Sarah Saturday-Friday. A good portion of this journey is frequently a musical adventure.

Fred Rogers is an accomplished musician who likes to set his television teachings to song. He has written and recorded such compositions as "When a Baby Comes to Your House," "What Do You Do with the Mad That You Feel?" and "I Like to Be Told," all of which have become standards on the undersized hit parade.

When the late Senator Robert Kennedy was slain in 1968, the world at large focused its attention on the tragedy swirling about the Kennedy family and about the circumstances surrounding the assassination. But Fred Rogers worried about the impact the string of political assassinations in this country was having on children, and he went on television to talk about what assassinations might mean to a child.

Beyond camera range, Misterogers and Fred Rogers look like nearly identical twins. The quiet speech and mannerisms, the low-key personality of Misterogers remain. Rogers likes to think of his life style as simple, a rather amusing contrast to the magnificent library in his Pittsburgh town house where we had our little talk and to the "comfortable" living room where two grand pianos are almost lost. Fred Rogers frequently writes and prepares his programs at his weekend retreat in Pittsburgh or at his summer home on

Nantucket, and it just goes to prove how elastic a word "simplicity" really is.

Romper Room (Syndicated, Monday through Friday)

Quite a few well-meaning people have cited this nineteen-year-old preschooler in the same breath with the word "excellent," but everybody is entitled to make a mistake or two. *Romper Room* is no little red schoolhouse. It is a series of little red schoolhouses. In fact, according to the chief schoolmistress, Mrs. Bert Klaster, there were at last count something like one hundred six in the States and forty-five in other countries. *Romper Room* is sort of a syndication of little red schoolhouses using a trade name — perhaps a little unusual for an educational institution — called Romper Room Enterprises, Incorporated. The headmaster, Mr. Bert Klaster, and his wife have established a school for *Romper Room* teachers near Baltimore and give a one-week degree in television teaching. Foreign *Romper Room* student teachers have a second week. The result is that wherever *Romper Room* is viewed it has a diecast look about it and some of the teachers appear molded like leaden soldiers. The scene, as they say, opens in a nursery room setting. The underlying philosophy behind the program seems to have been twofold: first, teachers, get in there and sell; second, your charges are little creatures who must be taught their ABC's.

Now, it is true that children love repetition and love to follow routines. And in theory this program purports to take advantage of that fact. The trouble is that many of the things repeated are inane and devoid of imagination. One blatant example comes to mind. The programs close with a "magic mirror" routine. Teacher holds up a mirrorless mirror and utters an incantation: "Romper, stomper, bomper-boo. Tell me, tell me, tell me true. Have all my friends had fun today? Have all my friends had fun at play? I see Steven having a special day." Then she says, "Please send us a postcard, and we'll send you one back."

Comments Harvard's Gerald Lesser: "Kids are treated like jerks. They are manipulated in a very stupid and dehumanizing way. The material they use is really inadequate for young children."

Until recently, the intricate blend of program content with commercial content gave *Romper Room* all the appearance of one tweedy sales pitch. The thread, however, seems to be unraveling, and the commercials are not quite so integrated or frequent. The credit in large measure may be due to an outraged group of organized parents who call themselves Action for Children's Television (ACT; see chapter 17). ACT officers quoted the Klasters as saying Romper Room collects from two-and-a-half per cent to five per cent on anything using the *Romper Room* name.

For about five years the *Romper Room* programs closed with a slide indicating they were produced in consultation with Dickinson College of Carlisle, Pennsylvania. Members of ACT have insisted that educators are often unaware that they are being exploited and have expressed the belief the *Romper Room* producers have been using a college name "to buy respectability." It was inconceivable to us that educators would blandly approve the stilted, completely uncreative format. In discussing the terms of the *Romper Room* contract with Dickinson officials, the conclusion we were left with was that the college had virtually no control over the program and had simply accepted free publicity. In 1969, Dickinson withdrew and refused further comment or explanation.

Later Romper Room Enterprises signed a contract with Hood College in Frederick, Maryland, because, in Mrs. Klaster's words, "Hood has a child development laboratory on the campus and because they see and test; we find this even superior to the help we were getting from Dickinson." Professor Charles Tressler of Hood told us a number of segments on the program needed changing, inasmuch as they ran counter to everything taught in Hood's nursery school. "One thing we made very clear from the beginning," he said, "was that we were not going to put a rubber stamp on just anything . . . If they are in the school business, then they'll have to be educating." On the question of teacher qualifications, Mrs. Klaster reported that all *Romper Room* teachers have *educational* backgrounds. In checking, we discovered this was not true. One teacher told us she had never taken an education course in her life! But the significant point is that there were other instances in which Romper Room Enterprises supplied answers to questions that were, if not deliberately untrue, certainly misleading. Mrs. Klaster's statement that Romper Room had *voluntarily* switched to Hood because that college offered more educational advantages failed to dock properly with the Dickinson statement that it was not the Klasters but Dickinson that had made the decision to sever the relationship. Mrs. Klaster had also implied that the Dickinson consultation sessions had been frequent and time-demanding. However, one Dickinson official reported that to his recollection the contract called for a minimum of two and a maximum of five sessions a year.

In January 1971, a check with Professor Tressler into the progress being made with *Romper Room* ended in a verbal cul-de-sac. Tressler belligerently refused to be queried about the program, referred to our telephone inquiry as "strange" and abruptly pounded his receiver in my ear. A second consultant at the college would permit no quotes to appear in print.

One big problem with *Romper Room* is that it takes place in a formal classroom setting. It is this kindergarten atmosphere that does not adapt to television because it prevents the building of a relationship between the teacher and the children at home. Professor Tressler, however, does not see the classroom setting as a problem. "It's my understanding they are really geared to the child at home," he says. But oddly enough the classroom seems to supply the economic rationale. It offers a selling point to a local station which can report to the FCC that it is offering "community programming." The implication here is that kids from the neighborhood can drop by the station and sit behind classroom desks, and the words "community programming" look just fine on an application when license renewal time comes around. At any rate, it helps to explain why a children's program that does not offer excellence can survive for years and be sold out around the country.

Digging for Pompeii

One of the notions we have heard expressed about the educational channels was made by a mother who remarked,

"I never let my kid watch educational TV. He's already getting enough education in school." Here is a woman who would flip on discovering that educational channels can also provide *entertainment.* Besides, in many communities the educational channels we pick up at home also carry programs called *in-school* television. No doubt the same lady would quiver at the very mention of the term in-school programs. These are carried during the school hours, but many of them are appropriate and entertaining to preschoolers, too. The in-school service, tuneable on home receivers, is often worth the extra spade work.

TELEVISION FOR THE SIX TO TEN

Television programmers are the first to admit they are not properly serving the middle range of kids, those who fall roughly between six and ten. We say roughly because we are talking here about a stage where children's growth rates vary so widely; six to ten forms a convenient age breakdown. In fact it is this variable growth pattern that provides programmers with their best excuse to cop out and shun their responsibility. The problem has been taken up in detail in chapter 13.

Wonderama (Metromedia, Monday through Friday and Sunday)

A talented performer named Sonny Fox guided this program through thought-provoking pathways that were delightful to tread along in the mid-Sixties. Today's syndicated version features MC Bob McAllister, who says his philosophy is that too many people on children's programs talk down to kids. Unfortunately, Mr. McAllister succumbs to his own lament. *Wonderama* now amounts to another giant giveaway, three hours full Sundays and one hour each weekday, offering lots of fun — all at the kids' expense. The appeal is strictly to greed. The same games are played *ad infinitum* to hand out toys and plug sponsors and potential sponsors. A drag race like this that goes on and on without additional content is completely unnecessary. Game shows should not serve as a ploy to shove merchandise at the kids whether they win or lose. But the idea of a creative game show *without merchandising strings* might be novel and provide a fine alternative.

Bozo (Syndicated locally)

When you take a look at Bozo the clown, you are apt to sputter in four-letter words. Words like "dumb," "ugly" and "vile" for openers. Bozo was somebody's bright idea of what a children's program should be. The ingredients for this hardy video weed help explain the end product: a booth announcer, preferably one who hates kids; a sprinkling of tasteless cartoons; leftover film clips that make no sense, replete with winged creatures or monster figures; a bagload of toys; and enough commercials to consume half the show time. Mix them all together, making sure to treat the young guests as morons and keep mentioning the names of the sponsors. This program is best observed with a basin nearby. *Bozo* is an outstanding example of when to turn the set off.

What's New (PBS, Monday through Friday)

Children in the six to ten group are reaching out to touch the world. *What's New* is dedicated to helping them. Its main failings result from an acute shortage of funds. It tries to be as wide-ranging and varied as possible, but often the budget does not allow for the shooting of required film. Often there is the need to fall back on stock footage. The show is woven together with a host, Al Binford. His performance comes across as pleasant, yet he fails to ignite much excitement. The lack of money also helps to account for the uneven quality of the programs, some of which are excellent, others of which are pancake flat. But on *What's New* they do try!

Discovery (ABC, Sunday)

Once upon a time NET's *What's New* was called *Discovery*. That title was sold to ABC, and it is not surprising to learn that today's *Discovery* is a more polished version of *What's New;* it is *What's New* with money. The budget allows the producers to take the show around the world to visit such sites as the ruins in Yucatán and to examine the waterfalls of Niagara. *Discovery* tends to become too much of a travelogue at times and could use a more personal approach. Of course, ABC manages to put the show in an undesirable viewing period, Sunday mornings. One might expect the network to find a slot for it during the week, inasmuch as ABC has little else to offer the kids aside from the cartoon block.

NEWS AND SPECIAL CURRENT AFFAIRS COVERAGE

A number of parents on our survey said that their children did not watch the news. We feel this is one of the areas where television serves the entire population best, and that most emphatically includes children. As soon as children are able to understand the bare bones of the news (as early as six, in some cases), they should be *encouraged* to watch. Some parents mentioned they were interested in keeping opposing views out of their living rooms. If you as a parent disagree with the viewpoint expressed, avoid playing the part of an ostrich. Let the children watch, but at the same time point out your disagreements and explain to your children the reasons why you disagree with the point of view given. You will be amazed how much they understand and how perceptive they can be.

No kid has to be asked to watch an astronaut walk on the moon. Our son, then six, was so involved with the first moon shot that he pleaded with us to wake him so he could have the real experience of watching Neil Armstrong make the first footprints on the moon. It is this sense of immediacy that television fills so well, and children and grown-ups alike respond strongly to it. Perhaps you are annoyed that the entire program schedule is bulldozed to make room for political conventions, but your youngsters may love it. The happenings portrayed by today's special events cameras are the paragraphs of tomorrow's history books. Those of us who recall the live coverage of the Army-McCarthy hearings back in the Fifties are still left with vivid impressions of those days. Not even the most talented teacher could reproduce the immediacy of those impressions. Again, this is another case where interpretations need to be made by the parents. But special events coverage can provide the best classrooms for the making of an informed citizenry.

16 ACTION FOR CHILDREN'S TELEVISION: APPLYING PRESSURE POINTS

"Children are not merely miniature consumers. They should not be exploited by television's great commercial system." Empty words spoken in frustration? No, angry words of determination, voiced over and over again, each time gathering momentum and force. First uttered by Evelyn Sarson and Lillian Ambrosino, both of Newton, Massachusetts, then echoed by their tough organization of parents called Action for Children's Television (ACT).

Evelyn Sarson and Lillian Ambrosino are not radical young students bent on overturning the country's free enterprise system. They are not part of some lunatic fringe — demanding that the television medium yield to a set of unnegotiable terms. Rather, Mrs. Sarson and Mrs. Ambrosino are two soft-spoken women who over the past several years have become frankly concerned about the influence television is exerting on their young children and on all children. Both ladies smilingly describe themselves as "Cambridge outcasts who have come to live in the pleasant intellectual community of Newton." Both of their husbands happen to work in educational television — one a producer, the other a programming official. Evelyn Sarson, a lively and bright, sensitive brunette with blue eyes, was born in England and has managed to preserve the charming lilt of her British speech. Lillian Ambrosino, also an attractive brunette, strikes you as needle sharp. She is a former journalist who still manages to find time to write even though she has a young family to raise.

Evelyn Sarson and Lillian Ambrosino want to upgrade the quality of television for young people. To do this, they have worked to organize clusters of parents into a viable pressure group in the hope of accomplishing through force of numbers what isolated protests in past years have never been able to accomplish. ACT is out to convince the television networks, local TV stations and television advertisers that children are special human beings, not simply consumers of goods. Their reasoning is that young children do not earn money and cannot write protest letters to their senators and congressmen. And so, say the members of ACT, children need protection from the kind of selling at which television has become so expert. In some way or other, ACT wants to remove the kids from the line of fire of merchandising guns. If Mrs. Sarson's and Mrs. Ambrosino's ACT group were to have its way, children's programs would move from the sales-oriented area into the public service area of programming, a sort of demilitarized, neutral zone. But it is unlikely that commercial TV decision makers would go that far, allowing the kids to have such an R and R camp set up, since television has learned so painstakingly how to make direct hits on young consumers with socko, zocko sales rocketry.

There is some evidence that the ACT members might settle for something less than complete surrender. Perhaps an agreement that stations would present their sales messages in blocks at the beginning and/or end of the shows.

Yet they are bound to meet resistance there, much of it of a guerrilla nature. There is likely, for instance, to be clamor from performers like *Romper Room*'s Miss Louise in New York, who tells us that breaks in the middle of the program give her needed time to wipe the perspiration from her brow after all her romping. But probably the biggest thunder will come from the networks and advertisers, who will insist that "natural dramatic" breaks are the only reasonable places in which to insert commercials. If the commercials are not in their accustomed places, TV officials are certain to ask, "Who would watch them *there?*" — overlooking their very own oft-quoted expression that kids love to watch commercials any old time, anywhere. But the members of ACT will not allow themselves to be intimidated, and they are quite prepared to swim upstream against the whole television current.

Action for Children's Television began in Newton in January 1968 as something of a neighborhood project. Shortly after the assassination of Senator Robert Kennedy, about a dozen young parents met at regular intervals in each other's homes to discuss what to do about excessive violence on television and burgeoning commercialism aimed at small children. Their concern was to find ways to work effectively towards quality television programming for youngsters. Largely through the energies of Mrs. Sarson, Mrs. Ambrosino and two other ACT officials — Mrs. Peggy Charren and Mrs. Judy Chalfen — the nonprofit group has been blossoming. It now can count more than three thousand members and supporters in thirty-six states. ACT has affiliated itself with the National Citizens Committee for Broadcasting in New York. The latter is working for higher quality television in adult programming, and ACT has become its official children's organization.

Parents who want to make changes often feel that networks, stations, and sponsors will pay no heed to their protests. That, of course, is an erroneous assumption, because television officials and advertisers are extremely sensitive to viewer criticism. Many times only a few letters are sufficient to bring the walls tumbling down; it is a phenomenon much of the public does not realize. Would organized parental groups, such as ACT, meet with furrowed executive brows? In some cases, perhaps, but enough pressure can bend even company policies.

Former CBS programming vice president Mike Dann: "It's the most healthy sign possble. Any pressure the public brings to bear upon any medium . . . whether it's public or commercial . . . if the people on one side feel a reaction from the other, that is the best thing possible. It's this vacuum, this void, this inertia, this lack of response that is the worst kind of thing."

NBC programmer Larry White: "Anybody who pressures for better programs is not making my life more difficult *if they have a program to offer as an alternative* . . . if the group is just not *against* [everything] . . . Most pressure groups today take the easy road for them . . . which is to be anti something. I have rarely seen what they are *for* . . . I would welcome all the help I could get."

Producer Jacqueline Babbin (CBS *Children's Hour*): "The way to get more and better television programs is to have people insist on it. I think in the final analysis the public is the one who can do it . . . very definitely, pressure groups can work."

TV and movie critic Judith Crist: "People just sit around and keep saying this is bad and that is bad, but they don't get off their butts. It does no good to sit around and feel helpless. If you go to a movie and don't like it, ask for your money back. If you don't like a television program, write to the sponsor of the TV show. Don't write to the programming guy so much . . . or if you do, you should say, 'I won't watch your network or station anymore because you are running stupid programs.' Then, write to every sponsor on the show and say, 'My friends and I won't buy your product anymore because you are sponsoring a stupid show.' And since TV is commercial, we've got to hit them where it counts. If you think it's a bad show, turn it off. You have to be vocal because they are bringing things into your house and you are entitled to have five good channels of entertainment and a variety of it. I feel this very strongly."

If anyone had any doubts about the effectiveness of organized viewer campaigns, he can draw an inspiration from Action for Children's Television. At 8:30 A.M. on September 8, 1969, Boston's CBS outlet, WHDH-TV, chopped *Captain Kangaroo* off the air at the midway point in the program; even while he had his mouth wide open, recalls Evelyn Sarson. Without so much as a word of explanation, WHDH-TV drew a final curtain down every day after the first half of the *Captain Kangaroo* show to make room for a locally produced show, *Bozo* the clown. The station later explained to ACT that it had stretched the morning news another half hour, inadvertently bumping *Bozo* out of the TV circus ring. But WHDH-TV wanted to hold on to *Bozo* primarily because, as station officials put it to Evelyn Sarson and Lillian Ambrosino, the program allowed for "community participation." A high and noble-sounding rhetorical phrase that meant kids could appear on the show. It is a phrase that looks most impressive on FCC license renewal forms.

Evelyn Sarson said, "We wanted to show WHDH-TV that we were *for* good TV; we weren't *against* anything." Accordingly, the ACT officials organized a letter writing campaign calling for the reinstatement of the second half of the *Captain Kangaroo* program. Lillian Ambrosino galvanized petition signing by a hundred nursery schools, and ACT officials even went so far as to picket the television station. This high-gear protest led to a confrontation between the ACT officials and executives of the TV station. At last, the five channel executives said the programming decision they had made would go on for thirteen weeks, after which there might be some rethinking on the entire matter. In the interim, WHDH-TV attempted to rationalize its decision in the *Concord Journal,* a nearby town newspaper, but ACT officials only continued the protests. On Monday, January 5, 1970, WHDH-TV yielded to the power of the ladies from Newton and reinstated the second portion of *Captain Kangaroo* in Boston.

At the outset, ACT decided that some ground rules had to be set up for children's programs. One of their basic tenets was and is that programs for youngsters should be noncommercial. They believe that the logical agency to supervise broadcasting practices is the Federal Communications Commission, but that it is structurally too weak at present; therefore, ACT is advocating a stronger FCC with more bite. "The commission has kowtowed to the broadcasters long enough," says Evelyn Sarson. "The FCC is supposed to be the public voice, but the FCC has said nothing, absolutely nothing. We want to tell the public the FCC is there to help them . . . and perhaps at last there may be some kind of reaction."

ACT began monitoring *Romper Room* because it was a typical children's program, had been on the air for many years and had been praised in some quarters. "A sample reaction," says Mrs. Sarson, "was something like, 'My God! What a terrible show!' and as we observed the program we noted the fantastic number of commercials — commercial contests, commercial toys, kids playing with *Romper Room* toys, and kids joining in commercial jingles." "And the books they were reading," adds Lillian Ambrosino, "were strictly the books they were selling." ACT then arranged to discuss the program with officials of WHDH-TV and were invited to do so over lunch. "They said if you think it's so bad," Mrs. Sarson told us, "what would be good? So we trotted back and put together a whole lot of suggestions." The suggestions in turn led to another meeting with TV station officials, this time, however, also with the producers of *Romper Room,* Mr. and Mrs. Bert Klaster. The Klasters kept insisting, Mrs. Sarson says, that the show was educational and so were the toys. ACT was especially concerned that the producers had duped educaters at Dickinson College into acting as "consultants" to the program. It seemed to ACT that the Klasters had bought respectability from Dickinson, that Dickinson, in getting publicity on *Romper Room,* was really unaware it was being used. ACT doubted that Dickinson had really done any real consultation work at all in the three annual meetings its staff had had with the Klasters.

In speaking engagements before educational organizations, the members of ACT warned professional educators they must guard against being used in promotional efforts by programs such as *Romper Room.* Until the Klasters promised reforms on their syndicated shows, ACT pledged to organize boycotts of *Romper Room* toys and protests against the show. Without explanation, Dickinson College terminated its contract with *Romper Room,* and Hood College signed a contract with the producers. Hood officials said they would undertake educational reforms on the program and had no intention of being a rubber stamp for the Klasters.

In the summer of 1969 Rhode Island's Democratic Senator John Pastore introduced for adoption amendment S.2004 to become part of the Communications Act. If passed by the Congress, it would prohibit challenges to radio and television licenses until the licenses had first been denied renewal by the Federal Communications Commission. Officials of ACT immediately asked to appear before the Senate Commerce Committee to express the organization's view. "We are most concerned," ACT director Evelyn Sarson told the lawmakers, "that this bill, if passed, would cut off public criticism at the crucial renewal period." ACT also testified that the bill does not deal with the essential problem of creating minimum enforceable standards for broadcast performance. The organization told Commerce Committee members that the Federal Communications Commission is handicapped in judging performance of a given broadcasting station because it lacks definitive criteria to do so. And ACT then presented to the Commerce Committee a list of criteria it had drawn up for children's programs, asking that it be read into the record. In concluding its testimony, ACT called upon the senators "to set up a general inquiry for the preparation of acceptable and enforceable standards for one of the most powerful industries in the country — before it is too late."

ACT decided that it wanted to meet with the executives of the TV networks to present its ideas on children's programming. Accordingly, officials of the group dispatched letters to the three networks asking for appointments. The outcome was almost predictable. ABC ignored the organization completely. NBC thanked them for their interest. CBS, represented by programming vice president Mike Dann and officials of the program practices department, cordially invited the members to meet with them on January 6, 1970. Among the changes proposed by ACT to CBS was that the network appoint a director of children's programming. Vice president Dann agreed with them, saying, "CBS should have a unit interested in children's programming, creatively constructed for the child." Following the conference, Dann said, "The ladies of ACT had made an articulate case and were among the most constructive and logical I have heard. The give and take was first rate. I have invited them back."

On February 12, 1970, the members of ACT submitted for consideration, and the Federal Communications Commission accepted, a petition urging a ban on all commercials on children's TV programs. In its petition, ACT called for three specific proposals. First, it wants no sponsorship and no commercials on any children's television shows. Second, it would like the FCC to prohibit any performer from using or mentioning products, services or stores by brand name during children's programs — or of including those brand names during any portion of the program itself. And third, ACT wants to have every TV station set aside daily programming for children totaling at least fourteen hours a week as part of its public service requirement. Further, it wants infraction of these standards to be grounds for license revocation. Throughout its history the seven-member regulatory agency has carefully avoided interfering in programming as an infringement of First Amendment guarantees of free speech. ACT is not intimidated by past history.

In the fall of 1970 ACT organized a new subdivision called ATAC, an acronym for Advice on Toys at Christmas. Prior to the holidays ACT initiated a new seasonal service. Through leaflets distributed at major shopping centers across the nation ATAC told beleaguered parents precisely how to cope with the sudden barrage of Christmas television toy commercials. At about the same time, Democratic Representative Fred B. Rooney of Pennsylvania called on the Federal Trade Commission to investigate the pricing, promotion and operation of the toy industry. Rooney charged the consumer is being "jet-cajoled and superpromoted by the worst collection of ultra-junk toys in the industry's history."

17 TV WATCHWORDS: A FLEXIBLE GUIDE TO BETTER VIEWING

When we consider it, the fact that a rigidly supervised child can spend as much as forty days a year watching television is a sobering fact indeed. It means that the vast majority who are not closely watched consume a great deal more time. And that fact underscores our contention that the real problem with television is that if uncontrolled it can be the biggest time killer in our lives. Happily, we do not have to federalize the process of tightening controls on runaway time; it can start on a very local level, right in our own homes.

Supervision is like the weather. Parents talk about it a good deal but very few do anything about it. Supervision, in the minds of some parents, simply refers to their physical presence in the TV room while the children are viewing. That, of course, is *not* supervision at all, but little more than passive observation. Some time must be set aside to help the child deal with television on his own level. All matters of discipline generally involve decisions about what is absolutely necessary for the child's good and about what we *believe* but are not certain may be good for the child. In the first instance, we must *insist* that the youngster comply with our wishes for his own welfare. In the second we are dealing perhaps more with matters of taste. Supervision is a matter of determining what kinds of television programs are appropriate for a particular child and which are not.

A parent should be observing his child's reactions to programs to see if the latter are appropriate from a standpoint of the youngster's age, emotional maturity, and curiosity. Obviously, what may be appropriate for one child may not be for a second, even if both children are chronologically the same age. If the parent attempts to avoid the necessary struggle that goes along continuously with supervision, then he enters into the realm of censorship, which presents quite another problem. Censorship and protectionism are based on the assumption that you can raise a child in a sanitized world, shielding him from the world's violence and ugliness. The censor tries to avoid a collision with reality; he also stunts the development of mature judgment and taste. Supervising the child's television habits involves erecting guideposts and moving them about as the youngster matures. It certainly is not the job many envision — that of hovering perpetually over the television set to pull out the plug if a sexy word of dialogue slips into the TV room. The parent who supervises properly helps set the scene for appropriate viewing and is near enough at hand to deal with problems or questions that may arise.

Many parents in our survey said they considered news programs inappropriate for children. We do not share this feeling, because television news serves to acquaint children with the world at large. Proper supervision would provide a necessary framework for understanding. Parents should not shield a child from the reality of the news but help him comprehend what is happening in terms he can deal with. At some point in a youngster's life — as early as five in some cases — watching the news on TV can be appropriate. The parent should be at hand to explain about the racial tensions that may have been seen or about tragedies of war. At the same time drama on racial tensions or war may be too stark for the child, and the parent might well consider it inappropriate for the youngster to view.

Many people have told us that they encounter no mealtime conflicts with television. The simplest solution, according to them, is to bring a TV set right into the kitchen or to give the youngster a tray and let him watch in the living room while the rest of the family eats at the table. All of the child guidance authorities we consulted concur with us that except under special circumstances television and meals do not mix well. Whether the adults choose to eat separately from the child or not, the television set should not be turned on. Mealtime should be a pleasant time; it provides the perfect opportunity for members of the family to communicate with one another. The togetherness provided by mealtimes is very important to the mental health of the family unit. Eating quietly and enjoying dinner without the accompaniment of TV can also provide relief from the day's tensions. There are, of course, exceptions to this general procedure when the family may decide to rearrange mealtime or watch television if an important special is on the air during the dinner hour. But inviting the television set into the dining room should have definite limitations.

Most parents are well aware that television can often serve as the child's rationalization to stay up. At a certain age — perhaps around four — getting to bed may be a fearful experience for children. This is when we are presented with all the "drink of water" routines. The mother or father may have to reassure the child that everybody will be around when he gets up the next morning. Beyond four or five, if the fear of going to bed persists with the insistence on watching TV, it may be an indication of some deeper disturbance that should be looked into. But, for the most part, when bedtime comes the parent should ask the child to turn off the set and go to bed. If the youngster refuses, the parent must simply be firm and turn the set off himself.

Those respondents to our survey who spoke of the possible conflict between homework and television said that if TV ever had any effect on school grades, it was generally for the worse. Homework and television should not be allowed to conflict. It is a simple matter to resolve if they do: *homework comes first,* and if it is not completed there should be no television.

Children have different thresholds of fear. Up to a point, most of them actually enjoy being a little scared. Watching the Wicked Witch of the West in the *Wizard of Oz,* for instance, may delight them in a scary sort of a way. Other programs may make the same children tense enough to want their parents sitting in the same room, but they still may want to watch. Beyond that, though, some events on TV may really induce fears and they may fidget, even if their parents are present, and even decide to leave the room. But each of these three levels differs between one child and the next. What may be a delightfully scary adventure for one child could frighten a second child to call for his parents, and yet a third to want the program turned off. The parent, who knows the child best, is really the only one in a position to know what the youngster can tolerate.

Television officials cannot say for certain that a particular program will not upset the children in the audience. That is a question only the parents of the children can be expected to forecast with any degree of accuracy. Again, it should be stressed here that parents tend quite often to project their own fear responses on to their youngsters. They may report that a program frightens their children, when what they are really saying is that they, the parents, get upset. In making judgments on a child's tolerance for fear, the parents should be careful to see that it is the child's reaction that is being gauged, not their own.

We learned from our survey that too few people actually make use of the television listings to plan program viewing. Scanning program listings well in advance can alert you to the better shows. Upcoming promising programs should be put down on the calendar. Even if parents are not home when the shows are on the air, the baby-sitter can help follow through. Specials create a sense of delight and anticipation for the kids, and noting them on the calendar in advance can ensure against their being missed. If a future program does not live up to its billboarded promises, parents can help children — especially the older ones — to develop taste by pointing out to them what they liked and did not like about the program. Program guides can be especially useful to teachers. Future lessons on a variety of subjects can be coordinated and built about the TV specials as valued classroom aids. Far too little use is being made of home television by most public and private elementary school teachers.

Parents who have not fully acquainted themselves with the rich ore of programming for children on the educational TV channels should plan an exploratory mission without delay. In the late weekday afternoons, between 4:30 and 6:30, while the commercial network officials are busy abdicating or alibiing why they are not offering afternoon programs for children, parents can tune in to the educational TV channels where there are two hours or more of uninterrupted, varied programs for young people, for preschooler and middle range child alike.

Most people we interviewed were strongly irritated by commercials aimed at children. Most of them expressed a feeling of helplessness in dealing with the problems commercials presented. If the parent feels the child should not have the advertised product, for one reason or another, he should not buy it. Under no circumstances should the youngster be allowed to tyrannize the parent so that the product will be purchased. If the parent decides he is offended by the commercial or does not approve of the product bought, he should write to the sponsor, the network and/or the station carrying the program and say so. Parents should not leave the judgments solely to the networks or to the independent station's standards and practices departments. Quite often the personnel of those departments seem to be out on their coffee breaks when many offensive commercials are being screened. The point to be kept in mind is that if the parent is disturbed by the commercial or the advertiser's product, he should not sit on his hands but make his anger known to the people who are making the decisions.

"Television frequently is more abused than used properly," psychiatrist Paul Syracuse told us. He meant that parents all too often conceive of the TV medium as a substitute for the kind of communication that should go on among mother, father and children. The people who reported that television helps keep the family together simply because it physically keeps everybody in the same room tend to think of TV as a communications substitute. Those who told us television could not bring a family together perhaps are missing an opportunity to use the medium as a positive force in the family unit. The really responsible parent can utilize television as a catalyst or source of common experience for the whole family. In this sense, the medium can serve as a jumping off point for discussion and open communication based on a shared experience. While not everything viewed on television is liked, certainly this common experience of watching together can lead to more cohesiveness and understanding of differing viewpoints among parents and children.

The positive power of television actually has no bounds. It can, if used constructively and prudently, help build more solid relationships between parent and child. The parent should work directly to engage the child in activities that TV points up. When books are read over the air, parents should take the children to the library to get the books and read to them. If the performer is constructing something the child is interested in, the parent can easily help carry over interest by gathering the required materials and constructing the object with the youngster. Performers like Misterogers often put out recordings that can help the child learn about matters that are important to him. Such recordings can often produce real communication between parents and their youngsters. Remember, these are the times when communication links are formed between the generations in a family. Television's greatest power is sometimes released *after* the set is switched off!

18 TV OUT OF SIGHT

A television network executive testifying before the President's Commission on the Causes and Prevention of Violence commented that it would take at least eighteen months to make any drastic changes in a network's programming schedule. The gentleman was partially correct. What he neglected to do was complete his sentence with the phrase "unless the networks are in a great hurry." When the television networks are fully motivated — not infrequently by an economic factor — changes can literally be made overnight. The commercial networks now appear completely shaken by the success of public television's *Sesame Street,* and they are not unmindful of the determination and compelling energies being generated by the growing parental lobby Action for Children's Television. After only four months of attempting to gauge the audience-building potential of *Sesame Street,* we are suddenly made aware of commercial television's abiding concern for children.

"We hope to help children, to stimulate and provoke their fantasy attitudes," remarks NBC vice president Larry White. "Our aim is to entertain, stimulate and educate," says ABC vice president Marshall Karp, breaking a long silence on the subject. CBS vice president Fred Silverman suggests that we are about to witness "stage three of a four-stage plan . . . it's part of our awareness that children's programming must get better."

The internal thrashing about within the commercial networks was no great surprise to the executive producer of *Sesame Street,* David Connell. "Assuming that this show is a success and effective," he told us in December 1969, "we would hope that it would influence commercial TV by showing them that it is possible to get an audience without having a supermonster. And we would hope it would influence those backers of public television by showing them that it does require time and money . . . and that you can't do good programming and attract an audience with a budget of a buck and a quarter."

On Sunday, March 5, 1970, the *New York Times Magazine* (Ferreti, "Children's TV Shifts to Fantasy and Quality") raised the curtain on the next act of programming for children which the networks collectively called the "fantasy and quality" phase. CBS compared what was to come in terms reminiscent of space age wonders. "Stage three of our four-stage plan," in the words of vice president Silverman, will comprise a series of two-minute informational programs to be shown during Saturday program breaks at 9:00 A.M., 10:00 A.M., noon, and 1:00 P.M. Eastern time. These mini-documentaries are being produced by CBS News and will "be on everything you can imagine . . . how-to's, government, geography, current affairs."

Around these featurettes CBS has added four new Saturday morning programs. Among the four is *Sabrina and Googley Goolies,* another animation starring Sabrina, the teen-age witch from the *Archie* series. "Characters from *Sabrina* will be the hosts of the educational two-minute programs." "*Archie* itself will become a fast-paced comedy-variety show, styled after *Laugh-In*." We noted that the quotes were all coming from vice president Silverman, not from CBS's supervisor of children's programs, Allen Ducovny.

The *Times* quoted NBC's vice president White as saying, "We've gotten away from conflict, confrontation and jeopardy situations." NBC has come up with *Tom Foolery,* an animated variety show patterned, we are told, after *Laugh-In.* Says vice president White, the program will use "material from Lewis Carroll, Edward Lear and Gelett Burgess." The network is also featuring an animated *Further Adventures of Dr. Dolittle,* based on the Hugh Lofting books. Live action is still popular at NBC, and the 1970–1971 season now has *The Bugaloos* in place of the *Banana Splits,* which have fallen into disrepute. That is part and parcel of the "What good ratings have you shown me lately?" game. *The Bugaloos* is a show about a quartet of musicians who get involved in weekly crises. NBC's prestige program is *Hot Dog,* based on one of the *American Rainbow* programs of the 1969–1970 season. "These will be dedicated to answer the 'Why, Daddy?' questions, like 'How do you paint the white line in the street?'; 'How do you make cartoons?'; 'Why does popcorn pop?' " And the network scheduled twelve more programs in the *American Rainbow* specials for 1970–1971. We noted that all the quotes were coming from programming vice president Larry White, not from children's programming vice president George Heinemann.

ABC suddenly is not interested in solely entertaining kids, but now worries about stimulating them and educating them. Says vice president Marshall Karp, "We try for all three, but we'll take two out of three. The problem with children's programs in the past was in content and execution. There was no literature, no theater, no content. The programs were boring and meaningless. We've tried this year to get literature into the programming. Why should the kids be denied content?" Actually, it appears they *will* be denied content until the fall of 1971 because ABC says it wants to make sure it sells all of its shows a year in advance. Meantime, let them eat cartoons.

ABC's proposed programs for the fall of 1971 included *The Reluctant Dragon* and *Mr. Toad,* the latter described as "an animated version of the old dragon tales and of the character in Kenneth Graham's *The Wind in the Willows.*" The network was also to feature something called *Scooper and the Double Deckers,* "a British series that combines elements of *Tom Sawyer, Huck Finn, Our Gang,* and *The Little Rascals.*" There was also to be a Jerry Lewis cartoon, *Will the Real Jerry Lewis Please Sit Down.* The ABC house-cleaning job produced a satire, *Lancelot Link, Secret Chimp.* This show has an all-chimpanzee cast with names like Dr. Strangemind, the Dragon Woman and Mata Hairy. It is dubbed "Swiftian satire." And let us not forget *Motormouse,* another cartoon hero, formerly a secondary character in an animation the season before. We noted that all of the quotes were coming from programming vice president Marshall Karp, not from ABC's new children's director Charles Jones.

Many cities around the nation are now carrying reruns of *Sesame Street* on Saturdays, and the astonishing fact is that the kids are selecting this content-filled program over the stream of vapid cartoons from commercial TV. So the battle for children's minds is taking place on Saturdays. But as far as we know there are no plans to show *Sesame Street* reruns on Sundays, too. With that effective competition out of the way, the networks feel sufficiently relaxed to shunt much of the dubious cartoon strip to Sundays.

Accordingly, we find ABC and CBS forging ahead on this course. NBC's vice president White has called Sunday mornings "local station time." It will be interesting to see how long NBC finds this policy a viable one to follow. The not too unlikely prospect is that we are witnessing the onset of a vast trade-off between a few quality program ideas and a whole virgin market featuring the same kind of program material we have been accustomed to seeing. There may no longer be the Saturday cartoon marshlands to tramp through. It is now likely to be a Sunday marshland, with network incomes following an upward sloping curve.

Television advertisers aware of the need to upgrade the general level of programs for children can provide the required leverage and momentum to force changes for the better. The Xerox Corporation, the Quaker Oats Company, Healthtex, and Gulf Oil Corporation have exemplified the spirit of integrity. They have shown selectivity in sponsoring programs of quality only. They have not joined the ranks of advertisers who will support *any* kind of program simply to keep their trade names before the public. The enlightened sponsor will risk lower-rated programs for the sake of quality telecasts.

Other sponsors, such as the Fisher Price Toy Company, are completely cognizant of the value problems that a commercial itself may present if their products are offered directly to a child. Their course is to sell the product not to the impressionable child but to his parent at a time when presumably just adults are viewing television. It is this awareness on the part of the advertiser of the need for better children's programming that can help bring about significant changes in the total picture of children's television.

When we spoke to professor Gerald Lesser, he expressed the hope that in the days ahead children's television will not only continue to show youngsters what the world is really like but how things *relate to them. Relevance,* which is so important, is an element that has not been much at home on the TV screen. Comments Lesser: "I would like to see children exposed to greater and greater parts of their environment — to the natural parts of it and to the man-made parts of it." Does Lesser feel that quality television in the future can possibly come from commercial TV? "Well, I think eventually it is going to have to . . . because that is where the money is. But I think it is going to require a lot more provocation first."

From a developmental standpoint, relevance can add *meaning* to the child's life. "Most drama today is unrelated to the drama of a child's activity," psychiatrist Irving Markowitz points out. "That is because there is a kind of contempt and feeling there isn't much drama in the life of a kid. But there *is* a drama to kids' lives. For example, getting a dog is one kind of an encounter. The way people react to what they are going to do about the dog. How the mother treats the dog. What it means to get the dog. The whole business of feeding him or not feeding him. What this means to the kid . . . what are his real feelings in the matter? What are his feelings toward his parents? All of these things are part of a child's life. All of them are his kind of drama."

The middle range child who is so difficult to program for can benefit from a new kind of television theater — relevant drama. The youngster should be able to view his own kind of drama and find identification within it. It should help him determine what he is and what he can be, what different roles he can adopt. Future television for children should be more consistent with children's lives. The medium should show the struggles kids have to take part in, how they resolve their conflicts.

Looking to the future of his area, NBC vice president of children's programming George Heinemann says he would like to present more stories dramatizing the social problems of the age. "I would like the child," Heinemann tells us, "to be more conscious of what is happening in his world today . . . what is going to happen next week . . . not the irrelevant things, such as what will probably take place in the year 2000."

In times charged with explosive sensitivities and careening change, youngsters must learn how to get a firm foothold on the world. They are inundated by technology's uncapped flood of facts and unknowingly rocked by swells of social shock waves. Television can momentarily freeze these fluid components of life. A television news program for young people, anchored firmly in understandable language and perspective, can help distill meaning from apparent chaos.

The typical television game show or TV contest attracts an audience, to be sure. However, the underlying motivational current that carries the children is churned up by greed. "How much can I bring back in the way of toys?" the kids ask themselves. "How much can the kids help move my merchandise?" asks the television performer. The televised game is not an end in itself, but a means to merchandising — one that leans heavily on exploitation of children in the studio and at home. The television officials have accepted the correct premise that youngsters love games, so the studio children are effectively marshaled to help sell merchandise that is "won." The TV "winning," of course, is largely an out-and-out giveaway; it is usually unnecessary to compete to win because everybody wins anyway. And the MC hardly ever forgets to "plug" the gift by its merchandising trademark. In a very real sense, the television game, as presently constituted, is generally an essential component of the very much bigger selling game. But we can still cling to the belief that television may one day mature. We can still hope it will allow the child's game to serve as an end in itself, furnishing a real sense of competition and pleasure. Perhaps television officials in the future will permit the game or contest to be based on true values of winning, minus the gimmickry and the brass ring and carnival atmosphere.

On occasion, television has granted children a glimpse at the performing arts. But certainly the door to good music, to art and to the dance is never opened very wide or long enough. Television surely has the capacity to prop it open, so that those who have never explored the world of the arts can step inside and have a thoroughly good look about. What these young visitors should have a chance to see are performers of their own age who are accomplished and gifted musicians, artists, and dancers. The television camera can pick up not only an electronic image, but the reflected halo of inspiration as well.

What does it mean to be an architect? A doctor? A steel

worker? An electrician? A nurse? A secretary? Television can show the children all about careers through drama and documentaries that are constructed on their own levels. Television officials should consider this as an area of program possibility holding out great potential. Again, the key word is relevance to the young viewers.

How many times have we all read descriptions by television officials of some forthcoming animated series that sounds more like a recipe than a cartoon! We learn each season that they are bringing out some lovable second-rate character (left over from the previous TV season) who will partake in adventures that are two parts Oz, a sprinkling of Felix the Cat, three jiggers of Hans Christian Andersen and a dash of Mary Poppins. The character's girl may wind up to be a witch who resembles Wilma Flintstone and who drives a Rolls-Royce. Why do television officials insist they must improve on children's stories in the name of "creativity"? Perhaps they will one day learn to accept the old favorite fairy stories and children's adventures without the nonsensical embellishments. They may even permit some good animated artwork to be used. Simple, pleasing stories with fine artwork would probably be more refreshing than most of us could take standing up. The network conception of program costs for children is often two-dimensional. Television officials either conceive of cartoons costing in the neighborhood of between $10,000 and $12,000 or think in terms of extravaganzas calling for a quarter of a million dollars. There is a happy economic middle ground worthy of executive consideration.

Television can bring historical figures into bold relief by raising them from the pages of the textbook into a situation with which children can empathize. This can be done by dramatizing the young lives of noted men and women who have made their imprints on time. The form such relevant presentation can take may be as varied as the imagination of the producer.

The competition for the dollar in children's television is obviously so acute that little consideration has ever been paid to the possibility of pooling resources to save money and provide reasonably good programming at the same time. The major networks regularly set up pool coverage for this very purpose when important news breaks anywhere. There can be no valid reason why they cannot apply the same pool principle with respect to covering some children's programming. For instance, if the networks were each to provide one hour of children's television every week on a different night in prime time (say 7:30 to 8:30 p.m.), it would automatically provide three hours every week of good programming for all networks. Such television could serve children in the middle age range. The advantage to the networks could be that costs could be pooled. A temporary truce might be declared — for at least an hour — in the ratings battle, and quality programs for young people might be given the needed opportunity to survive. In the event television officials consider this suggestion too impractical or radical to ponder seriously, they are reminded that parental lobbies are continuing to grow in number and influence. The day may well arrive when the networks and TV stations will be compelled by legal means to provide the kind of programming we are suggesting here.

There is some disagreement over the question of whether it is possible to train a child's television performer for his job. Many people insist performers are born, that training such individuals represents simply wishful thinking. Others like Fred Rogers (*Misterogers' Neighborhood*) and Robert Keeshan (*Captain Kangaroo*) have in the past spoken of workshops to train people in performing for children on television. Their feeling seems to be that in most communities across the country there are people — perhaps not now in any sort of performing occupations — who have the ability to influence and teach children. What they lack are mechanical techniques, which Rogers and Keeshan believe can be taught. But regardless of whether performers in quality children's television are taught or learn by intuition, they — together with the producers, writers, and animationists — must be first-class, talented individuals. They must be paid well and encouraged by network and station officials to do outstanding work in their respective assignments.

19 CONCLUSION

Television is without a doubt the most powerful mass communication force ever to be unleashed on mankind. It can reach out and instantaneously touch the lives of millions of people. To argue whether the medium is positive and vital or negative and destructive is as futile as debating the beneficence or perniciousness of air, water or fire.

As parents we have the ultimate responsibility of helping to mold the personalities of our children into thinking people. We can ill afford to have the medium take over that responsibility then later accuse television of implanting ideas or values we consider abhorrent to us. Our parental obligations demand that we play the major role in developing the young, impressionable minds that live with us by making certain we hold an enlightened control on the television our children view. The objective is to make the most valued use of the child's time and help him get the most out of his television watching.

One of the mistakes grown-ups often make is to assume incorrectly that children see things the way we do. Another is the tendency, especially prevalent among many television officials, to lump together children in different age groupings under the general heading "children." It is well to bear in mind that preschoolers do not see the world in the same light middle range children do, and the latter group who are roughly between six and ten years old do not see the world the way older children do.

Television network and station officials should not allow on the air commercials that take advantage of children by deliberately confusing reality and fantasy. The dishonest selling stratagem of sliding from program material into the commercial without delineation must be ended. Practices and standards departments should be more strict in evaluating children's commercials. Those that exploit youngsters through deception and false emotional claims should be banned. Vitamins and medicines must not be sold directly to children over television. With the increasing problems of drug abuse, it strikes us as imperative that television not aid in any way in making medicine or drugs appear appealing or attractive to youngsters.

Historically, the decision makers in children's television have been programming officials who have had little understanding of the psychological and emotional needs of their young audiences. If children's television is to emerge completely from the dark ages, its decision makers will have to be officials who understand and like children and executives who do not simply mouth the opinions of solely rating-conscious programmers. They must have the stature of vice presidents with full power to veto decisions which are not in the best interest of the children.

Articles written on children's television frequently exaggerate the network profit margins. Nevertheless, television officials should exert themselves to upgrade the quality of the children's TV product from the standpoints of both content and artwork. The commercial networks until now have been making healthy profits, because, they say, they have been showing the kind of program children want. But CBS's *Captain Kangaroo* has clearly demonstrated that a quality network program for children can operate in the black; and public TV's *Sesame Street* has shown commercial TV officials that a program does not have to be devoid of genuine content to draw large audiences.

Up until recently, television executives have been insisting that children's programming should for the most part consist of shows that entertain youngsters. The repetitive claim has been that the kids have had enough "education" in school and they are not interested in learning from television. *Sesame Street* exploded that popular programmer's myth by illustrating that the ideal children's program includes a blend of educational and entertainment elements. *Sesame Street* drew much attention to the potentials of public television, attracted parents who might never have heard of ETV, and did more than anything else in the history of children's television to shake up all three commercial networks. The hope is that the extraordinary, unexpected competition from public television may eventually move the commercial networks off dead center, in the direction of good programming. For the present, TV officials are at least talking about upgrading the children's divisions; now we will have to wait and see to measure performance against verbal promises.

The learning impact of television is greatest on the youngest children, because they are not as yet influenced by other factors which will later enter their lives, such as pressures of the peer group and schooling. The young people first learning to read (perhaps around age six or seven) may still be having some trouble mastering the printed page. Therefore they obtain the bulk of their informational requirements from television. But as they gain reading proficiency and their thirst for more detailed knowledge grows, children turn more and more to books. Television can help create reading readiness. The Children's Television Workshop has begun exploring the feasibility of teaching youngsters to learn reading by television. Those children who finally develop into avid readers are not held back by television. As they grow older (between ten and thirteen) the TV viewing habit normally begins to drop off and other interests in the child's life pick up in its place.

In the classroom, elementary school teachers report that television has influenced their teaching methodology. Children have become selective in listening as a result of television, and teachers find they must constantly develop new ways to hold the attention of the youngsters. In short, the classroom teacher is discovering she has to borrow many of the visual and auditory concepts of television and introduce them into her own teaching procedures.

Groups such as Action for Children's Television have forcefully demonstrated that organized groups of parents bent on changing television's wayward course can effect changes for the betterment of programs. The members of ACT have shown that if the television networks refuse to pay attention to them they will go directly to the Federal Communications Commission. And if they are then able to convince the FCC that reforms are indeed needed in the area of children's programming, an FCC regulation could well mean the loss of significant revenue to television networks and stations alike. Moreover, ACT is also urging members of the Congress to support their concepts of quality programs for youngsters. The pressure to make genuine reforms, therefore, is now foursquare on the backs of the three major television networks.

In truth, where does the responsibility lie for improvement in the quality of children's television? Is it the broadcaster's burden, since he has pledged to operate in the public interest and necessity over publicly owned airways? Or is it the responsibility of American parents to make sure broadcasters are presenting worthwhile programs? The obvious response is that it is a twofold responsibility. For the broadcasters responsibility means that they should not put dollars before children. For the parents responsibility means they are the guardians of the airways. The broadcaster is called upon to exercise his best judgment in presenting the highest quality product possible and to keep in mind at all times that he is dealing not with adults who can fend for themselves but with impressionable young people he has the power to influence. Yet no parent is relieved of his ultimate responsibility of seeing to it that his child is not exposed without guidance to false values and shoddy programs. His concern should always be that his child be well served by the television medium.

Bibliography

Arnold, Arnold. *Violence and Your Child.* Chicago: Henry Regnery, 1969.

Bandura, Albert. *Handbook of Socialization Theory and Research.* New York: Rand McNally, 1969.

———. "Influence of Models' Reinforcement Contingencies on the Acquisition of Imitative Response." *Journal of Personality and Social Psychology,* 1, No. 6 (June 1965), 589–595.

———. "What TV Violence Can Do to Your Child." *Look,* 27 (Oct. 22, 1963), 46–48, 52.

———. "Vicarious Reinforcement and Imitative Learning." *Journal of Abnormal Social Psychology,* 67, No. 6 (1963), 601–607.

Bettelheim, Bruno. "Parents vs. Television." *Redbook,* 122, No. 1 (Nov. 1963).

———. "Children Should Learn About Violence." *Post,* 245th year, No. 5 (March 11, 1967), 10–12.

Bromberg, Walter, and Gerald George. "Can TV Crime Shows Prevent Violence?" *Today's Health,* 47, No. 5 (May 1969), 87–89.

Carnegie Commission, *Public Television.* New York: Bantam Books, 1967.

"Commission Statement on Violence in Television Entertainment Programs." *National Commission on Causes and Prevention of Violence,* Washington, D.C., September 23, 1969, 1–11.

Crist, Judith. "Sex and Violence in Movies and TV: How Harmful Are They?" *Good Housekeeping,* 169, No. 2 (August 1969), 59.

Culhane, John. "The Men Behind Dastardly and Muttley." *New York Times Magazine,* CXIX (November 1969), 49.

Daley, Eliott. "Is TV Brutalizing Your Child?" *Look,* 33, No. 24 (December 2, 1969), 99.

Ferreti, Fred. "Children's TV Shifts to Fantasy and Quality." *New York Times Magazine,* CXIX (March 5, 1970), 79.

Gattegno, Caleb. *Towards A Visual Culture.* New York: Outerbridge & Dienstfrey, 1969.

Gesell, Arnold, Frances Ilg and Louise Ames. *Child from Five to Ten.* New York: Harper, 1946.

———. *Infant and Child in the Culture of Today.* New York: Harper, 1946.

Ginott, Dr. Haim G. *Between Parent and Child.* New York: MacMillan, 1965.

Gross, Marthe. "TV: Electronic Crime School?" *Christian Herald,* 88, No. 8 (August 1965), 15–19, 23.

Hickey, Neil, and Edith Efron. "What is TV Doing to Them?" *TV Guide,* 17, Nos. 41–48 (Oct.-Nov. 1969).

Himmelweit, H. T., A. N. Oppenheim and Pamela Vince. *Television and the Child.* Oxford: Oxford University Press, 1959.

Johnson, Nicholas. *How to Talk Back to Your Television Set.* Boston: Little, Brown, 1970.

McDermott, John F. "The Violent Bugs Bunny." *New York Times Magazine,* CXIX (Sept. 28, 1969), 95.

McLuhan, Marshall. "What TV is Really Doing to Your Children." *Family Circle.* 70, No. 3 (March 1967), 95.

Morris, Norman S. "What's Good About Children's TV." *The Atlantic,* 224, No. 2 (August 1969), 67.

Mussen, Paul, and Eldred Rutherford. "Effects of Aggressive Cartoons on Children's Aggressive Play." *Journal of Abnormal and Social Psychology,* 62, No. 2 (1961), 461–463.

O'Flaherty, Terrence. "Murder on Saturday Morning?" *McCall's,* XCVI, No. 12 (Sept. 1969), 73.

Palmer, Edward. "Can Television Really Teach?" *American Education,* 5, No. 7 (Sept. 1969), 2–7.

Schramm, Wilbur, Jack Lyle and Edwin B. Parker. *Television in the Lives of our Children.* Stanford, Calif.: Stanford University Press, 1961.

Shayon, Robert Lewis. "Violence: TV's Crowd Catcher." *Saturday Review,* 52 (Jan. 11, 1969), 103.

Sunderlin, Sylvia, ed. *Children and TV.* Washington, D.C.: Association for Childhood Education International, 1967.

"Surgeon General's Scientific Advisory Committee on Television and Social Behavior," *NIMH US HEW,* Washington, D.C., October 30, 1969, 1–14.

"Those Tired Children." *Time,* 84, No. 19 (Nov. 6, 1964), 76.

"TV's Saturday Goldmine." *Business Week,* No. 2083 (Aug. 2, 1969), 96.

Winston, B. F. "Rating the Influence of Television," *The PTA Magazine,* 63, No. 7 (March 1969), 6.

Wren, Chris. "Quality Clicks." *Look,* 33, No. 24 (Dec. 2, 1969), 102.